Houghton
Mifflin
Harcourt

JOURNEYS
COMMON CORE

Program Authors

James F. Baumann · David J. Chard · Jamal Cooks
J. David Cooper · Russell Gersten · Marjorie Lipson
Lesley Mandel Morrow · John J. Pikulski · Héctor H. Rivera
Mabel Rivera · Shane Templeton · Sheila W. Valencia
Catherine Valentino · MaryEllen Vogt

Consulting Author
Irene Fountas

JOURNEYS
COMMON CORE

Unit 4

Boy, Were We Wrong About Dinosaurs!
INFORMATIONAL TEXT
by Kathleen V. Kudlinski • illustrated by S. D. Schindler

EXEMPLAR

Lesson

21

Lesson

22

Lesson

23

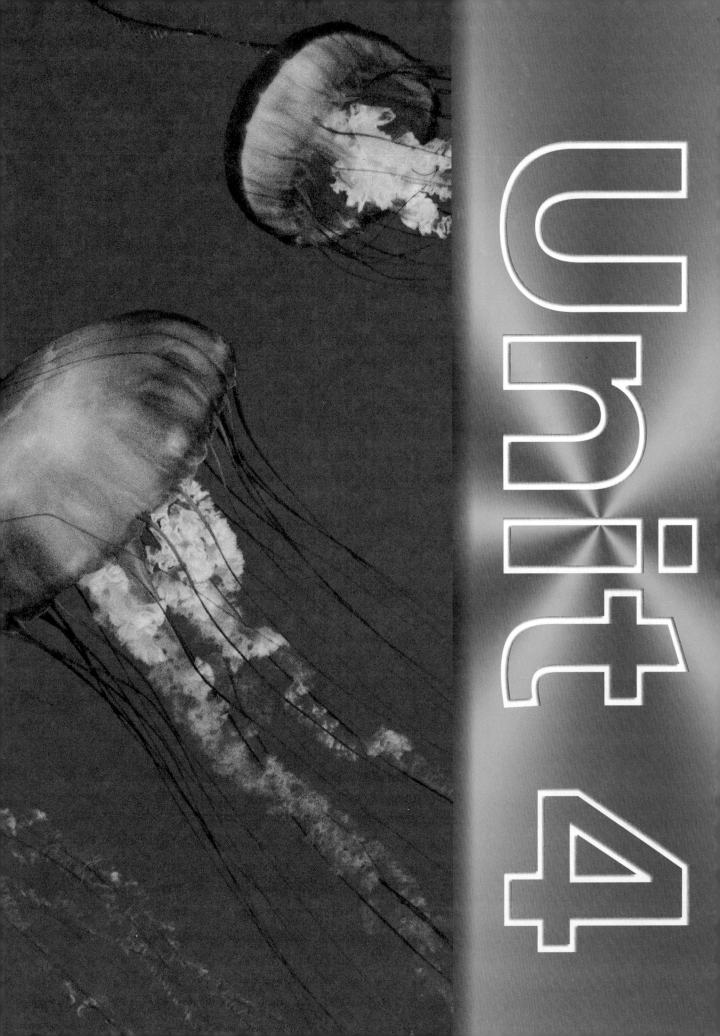

unit 4

Vocabulary in Context

☑ **TARGET VOCABULARY**

recycle
project
dripping
carton
complicated
pollution
rubbish
hardly
shade
global

Vocabulary Reader

Context Cards

 COMMON CORE **L.3.6** acquire and use conversational, general academic, and domain-specific words and phrases

1 recycle
When people recycle old bottles, the glass can be used again.

2 project
This garden is a neighborhood project. Many people work on it.

3 dripping
This faucet is dripping water. Each drop of water is wasted.

4 carton
A carton, or light cardboard container, can be recycled after use.

Go Digital

▶ Study each Context Card.

▶ Make up a new context sentence that uses two Vocabulary words.

5 complicated

One complicated, or difficult, part of recycling can be sorting plastic.

6 pollution

Noise pollution, or too many loud sounds, can be bad for our hearing.

7 rubbish

The more rubbish, or trash, people make, the more room it takes up.

8 hardly

Some light bulbs use a lot of energy. This bulb uses hardly any energy.

9 shade

The shade from this tree keeps the house cool in the summer.

10 global

Air pollution is a global problem. It affects people all over the world.

Read and Comprehend

✓ TARGET SKILL

Story Structure Each main part of a story builds on earlier sections of the story. As you read *Judy Moody Saves the World!*, pay special attention to details about the characters, setting, and plot events in the **first chapter**. Then look to see how the **second chapter** uses those details to continue the story. Use a graphic organizer like this one to help you connect the characters, settings, and plot in each chapter.

Setting	Characters
Plot	
Chapter 1	
Chapter 2	

✓ TARGET STRATEGY

Monitor/Clarify As you read, **monitor** or note any story details that are unclear. Reread or read ahead to help you **clarify,** or understand, what happens.

RL.3.3 describe characters and explain how their actions contribute to the sequence of events; **RL.3.5** refer to parts of stories, dramas, and poems/describe how each part builds on earlier sections

12

Conservation

When people conserve, they are careful not to waste resources. These resources may be water, food, and fuel to heat homes. As the number of people on Earth has grown, conservation has become more important. Recycling and reusing materials are ways to conserve resources.

It can be difficult to find a balance between conservation and the things people need. In this story, Judy Moody has a plan for teaching her family to conserve. She finds out that her plan is not as simple as she thinks.

ANCHOR TEXT

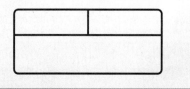

✅ TARGET SKILL

Story Structure Connect and compare the characters, setting, and plot events in the chapters as you read the story.

✅ GENRE

Humorous fiction is a funny, imaginative story that may be realistic or unrealistic. As you read, look for:

▶ story events that are intended to be funny
▶ characters that behave in humorous ways
▶ a plot with a beginning, a middle, and an ending

 COMMON CORE **RL.3.5** refer to parts of stories, dramas, and poems/describe how each part builds on earlier sections; **RL.3.9** compare and contrast themes, settings, and plots of stories by the same author

MEET THE AUTHOR

Megan McDonald

Once while Megan McDonald was visiting a school, some students asked her, "Are you ever in a bad mood?" This got her thinking about creating a character with lots of different moods. Judy Moody was born! Many of Judy Moody's adventures actually happened to McDonald when she was a child.

MEET THE ILLUSTRATOR

Peter H. Reynolds

Peter Reynolds and his twin brother started writing their own books when they were about seven. Reynolds has been drawing and telling stories ever since. After illustrating more than seven Judy Moody books, he feels like Judy Moody's family is part of his own family.

Judy Moody Saves the World!

by Megan McDonald

illustrated by Peter H. Reynolds

ESSENTIAL QUESTION

Why is it important to take care of our environment?

"Science, everybody," said Mr. Todd. "Let's continue our discussion of the environment. Rain forests everywhere are being cut down. When you take medicine or bounce a ball or pop a balloon, you're using something that came from the rain forest. And right here at home, malls are replacing trees, animals are disappearing, and we're running out of places to put all of our trash.

"Today, let's come up with ways we can help save the earth. Sometimes it's good to start small. Think of ways we can help at home. In our own families. And at school. Any ideas?"

"Don't leave lights on," said Hailey.

"Recycle your homework," said Frank.

"And cans and bottles and stuff," said Leo.

"Turn garbage into dirt," said Rocky.

"Yes," said Mr. Todd. "That's called composting."

Judy raised her hand, knocking her note to the floor. "Plant trees!"

"Don't be litterbugs," said Jessica Finch.

"I wasn't littering," said Judy, picking up the note. She crossed out the Finch in Jessica's name and changed it to Jessica Fink. Sheesh. Sometimes Jessica Fink Finch gave her the jitterbugs.

"Great!" said Mr. Todd. "These are all good ideas. Look around you—at home, in school, on the playground—not just in Science class. How can we help the planet? How can we make the world around us a better place? We can each do our part. All it takes is one person to make a difference."

One person! If all it took was one person, then she, Judy Moody, could save the world!

She knew just where to start. With a banana peel.

• • •

On the way home from school that afternoon, Judy asked Rocky, "Hey, can you come over and eat some bananas?"

"Sure," said Rocky. "What for?"

"Compost," said Judy.

"I'll eat two!" said Rocky.

In Judy's kitchen, Judy and Rocky each ate one and a half bananas. They fed the fourth and last one to Mouse, Judy's cat. Then Judy tossed all four banana peels into a bucket.

"Why don't we make a sign for the bucket that says TURN GARBAGE INTO DIRT," said Rocky.

"Rare!" said Judy. "Tomorrow we can tell Mr. Todd how we started to heal the world."

"Double cool," said Rocky.

"Wait just a minute," said Judy. "Why didn't I think of it before? HEAL THE WORLD! That's it!"

"What's it?"

"My Band-Aid. For the Crazy Strips contest! You'll see." Judy ran upstairs and came back with markers and some paper. At the kitchen table, Rocky made a sign for the compost bucket while Judy drew a picture of Earth with a Band-Aid on it. She wrote HEAL THE WORLD under the globe in her best not-in-cursive letters. Then she drew banana peels all around the world.

Stink came into the kitchen. "What are you drawing?" he asked Judy.

"Banana peels," said Judy.

"For the Crazy Strip Contest," Rocky said.

"And you thought bats were weird?" said Stink. "Bats aren't half as crazy as banana peels."

He looked at the empty bowl on the table. "Hey! Who ate the last banana?"

"Mouse!" said Judy. Judy and Rocky fell on the floor laughing.

"No way," said Stink.

"Just look at her whiskers," said Judy.

Stink got down on the floor, face to face with the cat. "Gross! Mouse has banana smoosh on her whiskers."

"Told you," said Judy.

"I'm telling Mom you ate all the bananas," said Stink. "And you fed one to Mouse."

"Tell her it's all in the name of science," said Judy. "You'll see. From now on there are going to be a few changes around here."

"We're making compost," said Rocky. "See?" He held up his sign.

"It takes like a hundred years to turn garbage into dirt," said Stink.

"Stink, *you're* going to be dirt. Unless you make like a tree and leaf us alone."

A Mr. Rubbish Mood

It was still dark out when Judy woke up early the next morning. She found her flashlight and notebook. Then she tiptoed downstairs to the kitchen and started to save the world.

She hoped she could save the world before breakfast. Judy wondered if other people making the world a better place had to do it quietly, and in the dark, so their parents would not wake up.

She, Judy Moody, was in a Mr. Rubbish mood. Mr. Rubbish was the Good Garbage Gremlin in Stink's comic book, who built his house out of French-fry cartons and pop bottles. He recycled everything, even lollipop sticks. And he never used anything from the rain forest.

Hmm . . . things that came from the rain forest. That would be a good place to start. Rubber came from the rain forest. And chocolate and spices and things like perfume. Even chewing gum.

Judy collected stuff from around the house and piled it on the kitchen table. Chocolate bars, brownie mix, vanilla ice cream. Her dad's coffee beans. The rubber toilet plunger. Gum from Stink's gumball machine. Her mom's lipstick from the bottom of her purse. She was so busy saving the rain forest that she didn't hear her family come into the kitchen.

"What in the world . . . ?" Mom said.

"Judy, why are you in the dark?" Dad asked, turning on the lights.

"Hey, my gumball machine!" Stink said.

Judy held out her arms to block the way. "We're not going to use this stuff anymore. It's all from the rain forest," she told them.

"Says who?" asked Stink.

"Says Mr. Rubbish. And Mr. Todd. They cut down way too many trees to grow coffee and give us makeup and chewing gum. Mr. Todd says the earth is our home. We have to take action to save it. We don't need all this stuff."

"I need gum!" yelled Stink. "Give me back my gum!"

"Stink! Don't yell. Haven't you ever heard of noise pollution?"

"Is my coffee in there?" Dad asked, rubbing his hair.

"Judy? Is that ice cream? It's dripping all over the table!" Mom carried the leaky carton over to the sink.

"ZZZZ-ZZZZZ!" Judy made the sound of a chain saw cutting down trees.

"She's batty," Stink said.

Dad put the brownie mix back in the cupboard. Mom took the toilet plunger off the kitchen table and headed for the bathroom.

Time for Plan B. Project R. E. C. Y. C. L. E. She, Judy Moody, would show her family just how much they hurt the planet. Every time someone threw something away, she would write it down. She got her notebook and looked in the trash can. She wrote down:

1 orange juice can
1 inside of peanut butter jar lid
1 plastic bread bag
4 broken eggshells
smelly yucky wet coffee grounds
3 paper muffin holders
2 smooshed Scarlett O'cherry juice boxes (and straws!)
½ Bowl of oatmeal

"Stink! You shouldn't throw gooey old oatmeal in the trash!" Judy said.

"Dad! Tell her to quit spying on me."

"I'm a Garbage Detective!" said Judy. "*Garbologist* to you. Mr. Todd says if you want to learn what to recycle, you have to get to know your garbage."

"Here," said Stink, sticking something wet and mushy under Judy's nose. "Get to know my apple core."

"Hardee-har-har," said Judy. "Hasn't anybody in this family ever heard of the Three R's?"

"The Three R's?" asked Dad.

"Re-use. Re-cycle."

"What's the third one?" asked Stink.

"Re-fuse to talk to little brothers until they quit throwing stuff away."

"Mom! I'm not going to stop throwing stuff away just because Judy's having a trash attack."

"Look at all this stuff we throw away!" Judy said. "Did you know that one person throws away more than eight pounds of garbage a day?"

"We recycle all our glass and cans," said Mom.

"And newspapers," Dad said.

"But what about this?" said Judy, picking a plastic bag out of the trash. "This bread bag could be a purse! Or carry a library book."

"What's so great about eggshells?" asked Stink. "And smelly old ground-up coffee?"

ANALYZE THE TEXT

Story Structure What happened in the first chapter that leads to Judy's Mr. Rubbish mood in the second chapter?

"You can use them to feed plants. Or make compost." Just then, something in the trash caught her eye. A pile of Popsicle sticks? Judy pulled it out. "Hey! My Laura Ingalls Wilder log cabin I made in second grade!"

"It looks like a glue museum to me," said Stink.

"I'm sorry, Judy," Mom said. "I should have asked first, but we can't save everything, honey."

"Recycle it!" said Stink. "You could use it for kindling, to start a fire! Or break it down into toothpicks."

"Not funny, Stink."

"Judy, you're not even ready for school yet. Let's talk about this later," said Dad. "It's time to get dressed."

It was no use. Nobody listened to her. Judy trudged upstairs, feeling like a sloth without a tree.

"I won't wear lipstick today if it'll make you feel better," Mom called up the stairs.

"And I'll only drink half a cup of coffee," Dad said, but Judy could hardly hear him over the grinding of the rain forest coffee beans.

Her family sure knew how to ruin a perfectly good Mr. Rubbish mood. She put on her jeans and her Spotted Owl T-shirt. And to save water, she did not brush her teeth.

She clomped downstairs in a mad-at-your-whole-family mood.

"Here's your lunch," said Mom.

"Mom! It's in a paper bag!"

"What's wrong with that?" Stink asked.

"Don't you get it?" said Judy. "They cut down trees to make paper bags. Trees give shade. They help control global warming. We would die without trees. They make oxygen and help take dust and stuff out of the air."

"Dust!" said Mom. "Let's talk about cleaning your room if we're going to talk dust."

ANALYZE THE TEXT

Theme Who is more convincing in the story, Judy or her family? What might this tell you about the theme of the story?

"Mo-om!" How was she supposed to do important things like save trees if she couldn't even save her *family* tree? That did it. Judy went straight to the garage and dug out her Sleeping Beauty lunch box from kindergarten.

"Are you really going to take that baby lunch box on the bus? Where the whole world can see?" asked Stink.

"I'm riding my bike today," said Judy. "To save energy."

"See you at school, then." Stink waved his *paper-bag* lunch at her. If only she could recycle her little brother.

"Go ahead. Be a tree hater," called Judy. "It's your funeral."

Making the world a better place sure was complicated.

Dig Deeper

How to Analyze the Text

Use these pages to learn about Story Structure and Theme. Then read *Judy Moody Saves the World!* again to apply what you learned.

Story Structure

Fictional stories like *Judy Moody Saves the World!* have a **story structure.** The structure has characters, setting, and a plot. **Characters** are the people in the story. **Setting** is where and when the story takes place. **Plot** is the order of events in which characters solve a problem. In a story with chapters, the structure also builds from chapter to chapter.

As you reread the first chapter, "Batty for Banana Peels," you can use a story map to list text evidence about the setting, characters, events, and the plot. As you reread the second chapter, "A Mr. Rubbish Mood," use the story map to show how events are connected and how the problem is solved.

Setting	Characters
Plot	
Chapter 1	
Chapter 2	

RL.3.2 recount stories and determine the message, lesson or moral; **RL.3.3** describe characters and explain how their actions contribute to the sequence of events; **RL.3.5** refer to parts of stories, dramas, and poems/describe how each part builds on earlier sections

COMMON CORE

Theme

The **theme** of a story is its meaning. It is the big idea, message, or lesson that the author wants readers to understand. As you reread *Judy Moody Saves the World!*, think about the story's theme. Look for text evidence that shows what the author is trying to tell you about people through what the characters say, do, and think.

Your Turn

Turn and Talk Review the selection with a partner to prepare to discuss this question: *Why is it important to take care of our environment?* As you talk, take turns exchanging ideas and connecting your own thoughts to your partner's. Use text evidence to support your ideas.

Classroom Conversation

Continue your discussion of *Judy Moody Saves the World!* by using text evidence to explain your answers to these questions:

1. What is Judy Moody's problem? How does she try to solve it?

2. Judy seems to think that her family isn't trying to save the Earth. Do you agree?

3. What would you do to convince people to conserve and recycle? How do your ideas differ from Judy Moody's plan?

WRITE ABOUT READING

Response Saving the world isn't an easy job. Imagine that you are Judy's friend. What advice would you give her about her plans to protect the environment? Write your ideas in an e-mail to Judy. Be sure to use a proper e-mail format.

Writing Tip

State the purpose of your e-mail in the first sentence. Then write your ideas along with reasons to support them. Check that every sentence is complete.

☑ **GENRE**

Humorous fiction is a funny, made-up story that may or may not seem realistic.

☑ **TEXT FOCUS**

Some authors write **series books** so that they can tell many different stories about the same characters.

RL.3.9 compare and contrast themes, settings, and plots of stories by the same author; **RL.3.10** read and comprehend literature

My Smelly Pet

from

Judy Moody

by Megan McDonald

illustrated by Peter H. Reynolds

For a collage about herself, Judy Moody needs to show her favorite pet. Judy's family has one pet, an old cat named Mouse. Judy said that Mouse can't be her *favorite* pet if she is their only pet. Her parents agree to take her to the pet store.

At the store, Judy finds a strange little plant. The store assistant explains that it is a Venus flytrap. Even though it is a plant, it eats insects such as flies and ants. Back at home, Judy and her little brother, Stink, feed the plant too much. Judy takes it to school the next day anyway, hoping that it will digest its meal in time for Share and Tell.

Tomorrow morning came. The jaws were still closed. Judy tried teasing it with a brand new ant. "Here you go," she said in her best squeaky baby voice. "You like ants, don't you?" The jaws did not open one tiny centimeter. The plant did not move one trigger hair.

Judy gave up. She carefully lodged the plant in the bottom of her backpack. She'd take it to school, stinky, smelly glob of hamburger and all.

On the bus, Judy showed Rocky her new pet. "I couldn't wait to show everybody how it eats. Now it won't even move. And it smells."

"Open Sesame!" said Rocky, trying some magic words. Nothing happened.

"Maybe," said Rocky, "the bus will bounce it open."

"Maybe," said Judy. But even the bouncing of the bus did not make her new pet open up.

"If this thing dies, I'm stuck with Mouse for MY FAVORITE PET," Judy said.

Mr. Todd said first thing, "Okay, class, take out your Me collage folders. I'll pass around old magazines, and you can spend the next half-hour cutting out pictures for your collages. You still have over three weeks, but I'd like to see how everybody's doing."

Her Me collage folder! Judy had been so busy with her new pet, she had forgotten to bring her folder to school.

Judy Moody sneaked a peek at Frank Pearl's folder. He had cut out pictures of macaroni (favorite food?), ants (favorite pet?), and shoes. Shoes? Frank Pearl's best friend was a pair of shoes?

Judy looked down at the open backpack under her desk. The jaws were still closed. Now her whole backpack was smelly. Judy took the straw from her juice box and poked at the Venus flytrap. No luck. It would never open in time for Share and Tell!

"Well?" Frank asked.

"Well, what?"

"Are you going to come?"

"Where?"

"My birthday party. A week from Saturday. All the boys from our class are coming. And Adrian and Sandy from next door."

Judy Moody did not care if the president himself was coming. She sniffed her backpack. It stunk like a skunk!

"What's in your backpack?" Frank asked.

"None of your beeswax," Judy said.

"It smells like dead tuna fish!" Frank Pearl said. Judy hoped her Venus flytrap would come back to life and bite Frank Pearl before he ever had another birthday.

Mr. Todd came over. "Judy, you haven't cut out any pictures. Do you have your folder?"

"I did—I mean—it was—then—well—no," said Judy. "I got a new pet last night."

"Don't tell me," said Mr. Todd. "Your new pet ate your Me collage folder."

"Not exactly. But it did eat one dead fly and one live ant. And then a big glob of . . ."

"Next time try to remember to bring your folder to school, Judy. And please, everyone, keep homework away from animals!"

"My new pet's not an animal, Mr. Todd," Judy said. "And it doesn't eat homework. Just bugs and raw hamburger." She pulled the Venus flytrap from her backpack. Judy could not believe her eyes! Its arm was no longer droopy. The stuck trap was now wide open, and her plant was looking hungry.

"It's MY FAVORITE PET," said Judy. "Meet Jaws!"

Compare Texts

Compare Judy's Adventures The two Judy Moody stories you read are alike in some ways and different in other ways. With a partner, discuss the characters, the setting, the plot, and the theme of each story. Then list three similarities and three differences.

Talk About Helping In *Judy Moody Saves the World!*, Judy Moody reduces the use of rain forest products. Take turns in a group telling about something you might do to help the environment. Ask questions to learn more about each person's ideas.

Connect to Social Studies Research the locations of rain forests around the world. Show the class the rain forests' locations by pointing to them on a map.

Go Digital

COMMON CORE **RL.3.9** compare and contrast themes, settings, and plots of stories by the same author; **W.3.7** conduct short research projects that build knowledge about a topic; **SL.3.1c** ask questions to check understanding, stay on topic, link comments to others' remarks; **SL.3.1d** explain own ideas and understanding in light of the discussion

L.3.1a explain the function of nouns, pronouns, verbs, adjectives, and adverbs; **L.3.1f** ensure subject-verb and pronoun-antecedent agreement

Grammar

What Are Adjectives and Articles? An **adjective** is a word that describes, or tells about, a noun. Some adjectives tell what kind. Some tell how many.

The words *a, an,* and *the* are called **articles.** They tell which noun. Use *a* and *an* with singular nouns. Use *an* before a noun that begins with a vowel. Use *the* with both singular and plural nouns. *The* is a definite article that tells about a specific, definite thing.

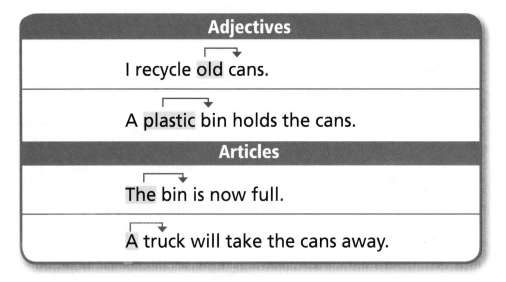

Adjectives
I recycle old cans.
A plastic bin holds the cans.

Articles
The bin is now full.
A truck will take the cans away.

Try This! **Work with a partner. Read each sentence aloud. Identify the adjective in each sentence. Identify any articles you see.**

1. A loud noise awakened Tanya.

2. Giant bottles were singing in Tanya's room!

3. They were telling Tanya to recycle old bottles.

4. Today she will recycle fifty bottles.

5. She will put them in the blue bin.

You can make your writing smooth and clear if you combine some sentences. If two short sentences tell about one noun, try combining the sentences by moving an adjective.

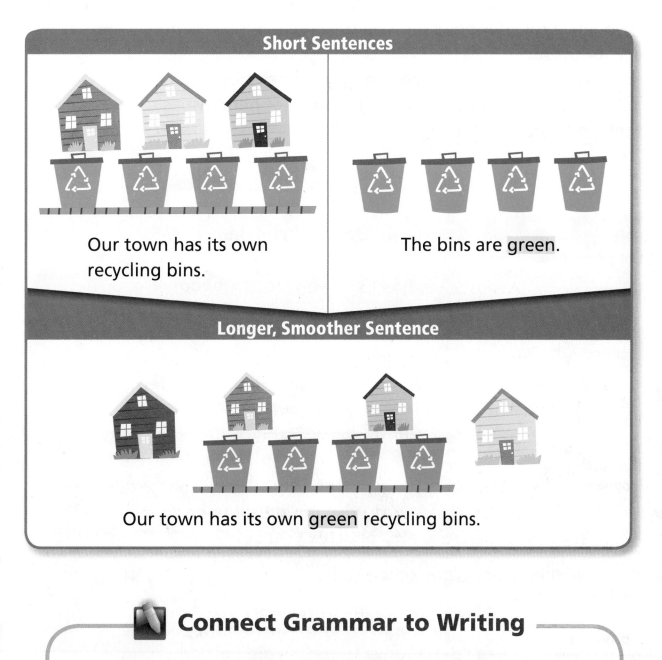

Short Sentences

Our town has its own recycling bins.

The bins are green.

Longer, Smoother Sentence

Our town has its own green recycling bins.

Connect Grammar to Writing

As you revise your persuasive letter, try moving adjectives to combine sentences.

Opinion Writing

✔ **Ideas**   In *Judy Moody Saves the World!*, Judy gives strong reasons for saving trees. When you write and revise your **persuasive letter**, think about the reasons you give for your opinion. Will they seem important to your reader?

Bianca wrote a letter persuading her neighbors to do more walking. Later, she changed some of her reasons to make them stronger.

Writing Traits Checklist

✔ **Ideas**
   Did I introduce the topic and give my opinions?

✔ **Organization**
   Did I use correct letter form?

✔ **Word Choice**
   Did I use polite language?

✔ **Voice**
   Did I write in a positive tone?

✔ **Sentence Fluency**
   Did I combine short, choppy sentences?

✔ **Conventions**
   Did I use commas correctly? Did I write neatly in cursive?

Revised Draft

Dear Oak Hill Neighbors,

   Let's take steps to become a

healthier community. Walking steps!

~~If we walk more and drive less, we~~ ʸ

~~will all be better off.~~ ʸ Walking may

                      it's great exercise
take longer than driving, but ʌ ~~at least~~
   that you can do all year round.
ʌ ~~you don't have to stop for traffic lights.~~

             important
Another ʌreason to walk is for cleaner
          Car fumes hurt our lungs and heart.
air. ʌ ~~That is an important reason.~~

Final Copy

182 Foster Street
Bentley, MO 23456
April 8, 2014

Oak Hill Neighborhood Organization
15 Cherry Street
Bentley, MO 23456

Dear Oak Hill Neighbors,

Let's take steps to become a healthier community. Walking steps! Walking may take longer than driving, but it's great exercise that you can do all year round. Another important reason to walk is for cleaner air. Car fumes hurt our lungs and heart. Finally, walking is relaxing because you can chat with neighbors and enjoy being outside. Let's all walk more for a healthier, happier community.

Sincerely,
Bianca Romano

Reading as a Writer

Which sentence states Bianca's opinion? Are the reasons important? Where can you give stronger reasons in your letter?

I gave strong reasons for my opinion. I also combined two short sentences.

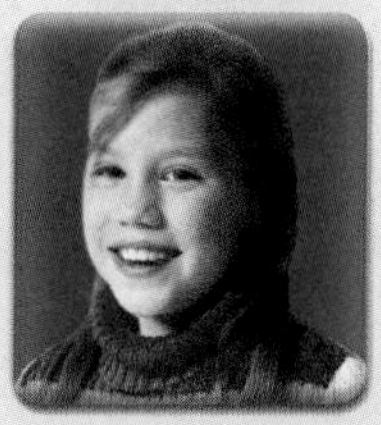

☑ **TARGET VOCABULARY**

fossils
clues
remains
prove
evidence
skeletons
uncovering
buried
fierce
location

Vocabulary   Context
Reader   Cards

L.3.6 acquire and use conversational, general academic, and domain-specific words and phrases

Vocabulary in Context

① fossils
This man has found dinosaur fossils. He will learn a lot from the old bones.

② clues
Fossils give clues that help scientists solve mysteries about dinosaurs.

③ remains
These are the remains of a large dinosaur. One bone is all that is left.

④ prove
Scientists are trying to prove, or show, that dinosaurs and birds are related.

▶ Study each Context Card.

▶ Ask a question that uses one of the Vocabulary words.

⑤ evidence

Egg fossils give evidence, or facts, about how dinosaurs raised their young.

⑥ skeletons

Scientists rarely find whole dinosaur skeletons like this one.

⑦ uncovering

Uncovering fossils takes time. The soil must be removed from around them.

⑧ buried

Many dinosaur bones were buried, or covered, in mud.

⑨ fierce

Many people think of dinosaurs as fierce animals that fought all the time.

⑩ location

Sometimes many dinosaur bones are found in the same location.

Read and Comprehend

Go Digital

✓ TARGET SKILL

Conclusions As you read *The Albertosaurus Mystery,* look for clues, or text evidence, that can help you understand the topic. You can use this text evidence along with your own ideas to make smart guesses about the topic that the author does not state. When you do this, you are drawing **conclusions.** Use a graphic organizer like this one to list text details that help you reach conclusions.

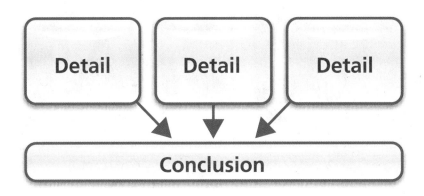

| Detail | Detail | Detail |

Conclusion

✓ TARGET STRATEGY

Visualize As you read *The Albertosaurus Mystery,* pay close attention to text evidence that helps you **visualize,** or create mental pictures of, what the author describes.

COMMON CORE

RI.3.1 ask and answer questions to demonstrate understanding, referring to the text

Fossils

Our world is full of mysteries. Earth science, or the study of the earth, helps explain some of these mysteries. For example, studying the earth has led scientists to fossils. Fossils are hints of plants or animals that have lived a very long time ago. A fossil can show the shape of a leaf, or it can be a bone that has turned into stone.

When scientists find fossils, they may or may not know what the ancient living plant or animal was. Sometimes a fossil is a clue in a new mystery. In *The Albertosaurus Mystery*, you'll see how scientists used fossils to answer an important question about how dinosaurs lived.

ANCHOR TEXT

The ALBERTOSAURUS MYSTERY

☑ TARGET SKILL

Conclusions Use text evidence along with what you already know to draw conclusions.

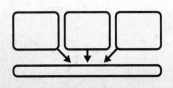

☑ GENRE

Informational text gives information about a topic. As you read, look for:

- ▶ headings that tell what each section is about
- ▶ photographs and captions
- ▶ graphics such as maps that help explain the topic

RI.3.1 ask and answer questions to demonstrate understanding, referring to the text; **RI.3.6** distinguish own point of view from that of the author; **RI.3.10** read and comprehend informational texts

MEET THE AUTHOR

T. V. PADMA

T. V. Padma, whose full name is Dr. Padma Venkatraman, has a lot of different interests. She loves science, math, nature, animals, space, the ocean, fossils, music, history, and poetry. Padma was born in India. She lives in Rhode Island now, where she enjoys canoeing, hiking, and horseback riding.

The ALBERTOSAURUS MYSTERY

FOSSIL HUNTERS

Philip Currie's Hunt in the Badlands

by T. V. Padma

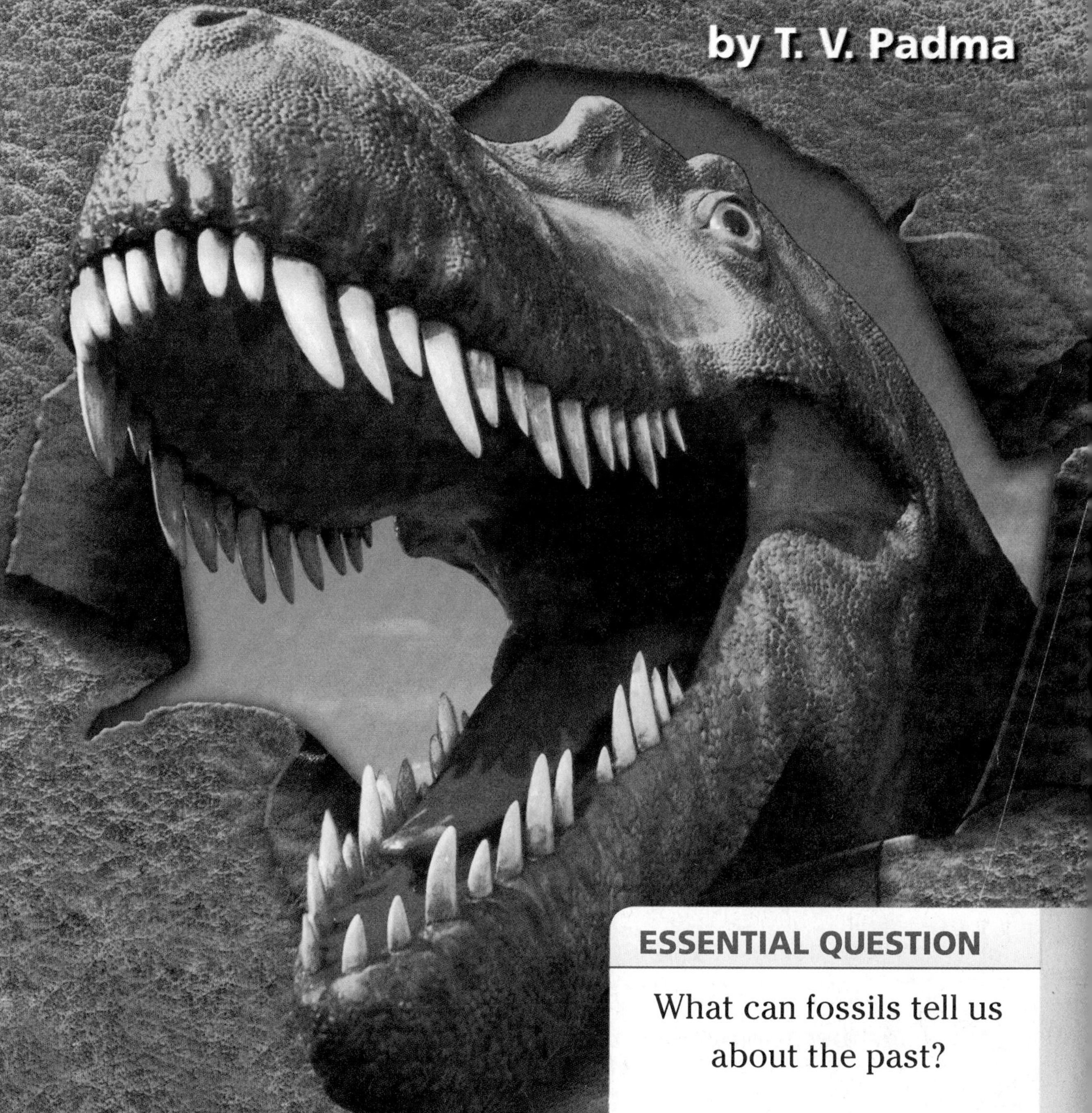

ESSENTIAL QUESTION

What can fossils tell us about the past?

Searching Without a Map

Many fossils are buried in Canada's badlands. More than 40 kinds of dinosaurs once lived there.

Philip Currie was thirsty and tired. It was one of the hottest summer days of 1997. He and his team were looking for fossils that belonged to a dinosaur called *Albertosaurus* (al bur toh SOHR uhs).

The badlands of western Canada are full of hills. Philip didn't know which hill held Brown's fossils.

Almost 90 years earlier, a famous fossil hunter named Barnum Brown had found a fossil field in western Canada's badlands. Many albertosaurs were buried in it. Philip was trying to find this place again.

It was like looking for a needle in a haystack. Brown had not made a map or written down where he had found the fossils. Philip had few clues—just some notes and four old photos.

Discovery!

The team was running out of water. Everyone except Philip went back to the camp. He continued on with the search. Sand flies and mosquitoes bit him. His head hurt.

Philip had seen the remains of Brown's campsite earlier in the day. He knew the bones must be close.

Philip was trying to find the location of *Albertosaurus* fossils shown in Brown's old photograph.

All alone, Philip climbed another hill. He stopped to hold up a photo. It looked just like the scene in front of him. He also could see that years ago someone had dug into the rock there. Philip had found Brown's bone bed!

Brown's photo was old, but Philip could see that the hills still looked the same.

Holes or cuts in rocky hills are clues that someone might have dug there before.

Barnum the Bone Hunter

Barnum Brown grew up in Kansas in the late 1800s. His family dug and sold coal. Young Barnum saw his first fossil when the family plow accidentally pulled one out of the ground.

Brown went on to study fossils. He found that he liked digging up bones more than learning about them in class. So he left Columbia University to become a bone hunter for the American Museum of Natural History in New York City.

Brown was very good at finding fossils. Henry Fairfield Osborn, the head of the museum, joked that Brown could "smell fossils." News writers called him "Mr. Bones."

At the American Museum of Natural History in New York City, Brown helped put together the bones he found.

Finding the First T. rex

In 1908, Brown found this *T. rex* skeleton. It can be seen at the American Museum of Natural History.

In the early 1900s, Brown dug up *Tyrannosaurus rex* (tuh ran uh SOHR uhs REKS) skeletons, first in Wyoming, and later in Montana. These were the first *T. rex* skeletons ever found.

For several years, Brown returned to Montana to dig for fossils. The bones he found there were often stuck in hard rock. He sometimes used dynamite to get them out.

Then in 1910 a terrible thing happened in Brown's life. His wife died. Brown tried to forget his sadness by hunting for more fossils. He rafted down Red Deer River Canyon in Canada. He camped in the area, and looked for bones. Soon, Brown made a surprising discovery.

Finding Many Meat-Eaters

In Canada, Brown found a place where many skeletons were buried. The skeletons belonged to *Albertosaurus*, a large meat-eating dinosaur. It was the first time anyone had found the bones of so many meat-eating dinosaurs in the same spot.

Brown dug up some of the bones. He wrote only a few lines about his find but didn't say how unusual it was. He didn't say why he thought so many individuals of the same species were together. He didn't tell what this discovery might mean.

The *Albertosaurus* bones were sent to the museum and put away. There they lay in a basement storage room for many years with other dinosaur fossils.

Albertosaurus got its name because the dinosaur's fossils were first found in Alberta, Canada.

A Fierce Family

Albertosaurus was part of a family of fierce, meat-eating dinosaurs called tyrannosaurids. *Tyrannosaurus rex* was also part of this family.

Albertosaurus was smaller than *Tyrannosaurus rex*, but it was strong. *Albertosaurus* could see and smell well. It had many sharp teeth. Its huge, powerful jaws could crush bone.

Like *Tyrannosaurus rex*, *Albertosaurus* lived and hunted alone. At least, that's what paleontologists thought. One man was about to change their thinking, however. He had some ideas about these ancient creatures.

ANALYZE THE TEXT

Point of View What does the author think about the bones that Barnum Brown found? What do you think?

Tyrannosaurus rex was about 40 feet (12 meters) long. *Albertosaurus* was about 30 feet (9 meters) long.

Philip Currie's Question

In 1976, Philip Currie read what Brown wrote about the site full of albertosaurs. At that time, most paleontologists thought tyrannosaurids lived alone. If so, asked Philip, why were many of these animals buried together? Had they died together? Had they lived together?

Some plant-eating dinosaurs had lived in groups. Maybe some of the meat-eaters that hunted them did, too, thought Philip. After all, big groups of animals were hard to hunt alone. Maybe albertosaurs hunted in packs.

Philip was busy learning about many kinds of fossils and dinosaurs, however. He put his questions away for many years, just as Brown had put away his fossils.

Albertosaurus had about seventy teeth in its gigantic jaws.

The Bones in the Basement

◄ The American Museum of Natural History, where Brown's *Albertosaurus* fossils were stored.

This fossil foot bone from an *Albertosaurus* was first discovered by Barnum Brown in Alberta, Canada, and then rediscovered by Philip Currie in New York City. ▶

Philip thought about his questions again 20 years later. This time, however, something happened that made him hunt for answers.

Philip came across some *Albertosaurus* bones in the basement of the American Museum of Natural History— the museum where Barnum Brown had worked. He could tell that the bones were from the badlands in Canada where Brown had been searching for fossils.

Philip saw that Brown had found at least nine albertosaurs in one spot. He also saw that Brown had taken only a few bones from each animal. More bones were still buried in the badlands, waiting to be discovered.

The Bones in the Badlands

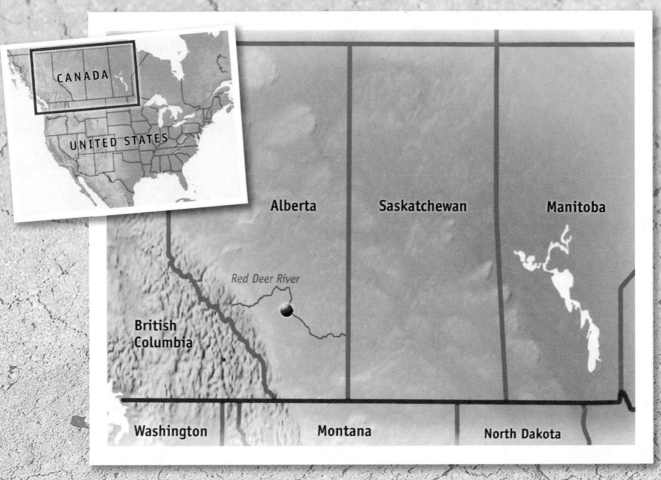

Place where Philip rediscovered the *Albertosaurus*
fossil site first found by Barnum Brown

Philip discovered more than bones at the museum.
He also found Brown's field notes and a photo of
Brown's site. Using these clues, Philip was able to find
the bone bed.

ANALYZE THE TEXT

Conclusions Why did finding so many
albertosaur fossils in one place make the team
question whether albertosaurs had lived alone?

Locating the spot was just the first step, however. Philip and his team worked for months to dig out each fossil. At least 22 albertosaurs were buried in the rock.

After the work was done, a new question came up. Did finding many fossils together prove that the animals had lived, died, and even hunted as a group?

Philip uncovering *Albertosaurus* bones in the badlands

In the days of Barnum Brown, fossil hunters were not always able to keep good records. Today, paleontologists carefully record their finds with photographs, drawings, maps, and reports.

What May Have Happened

Philip knew there could be other reasons for the fossils being together. Many of these ideas only brought up more questions, however.

For example, the albertosaurs could have died in quicksand. Yet different kinds of dinosaurs could die in quicksand. Philip had found the fossils of only one kind— *Albertosaurus*.

Maybe the albertosaurs had gathered to lay eggs. If so, however, the fossils should have been about the same age and size. Yet Philip had found small, young animals as well as large, old animals.

Philip's hunt had ended. Yet he needed more evidence to show that the meat-eaters had lived together.

A reconstructed nest of fossilized dinosaur eggs

Scientists know that dinosaurs laid eggs because fossil eggs of several kinds of dinosaurs have been found.

More Groups of Meat-Eaters

Rodolfo Coria uncovers teeth on a huge dinosaur jawbone.

More evidence came when a paleontologist named Rodolfo Coria phoned Philip. Coria was calling from Argentina. He also had found a spot where a group of meat-eating dinosaurs was buried. So perhaps meat-eaters did live in groups after all.

Scientists found more places with groups of meat-eating dinosaurs. These places were all over—Arizona, Montana, South Dakota, Utah, Mongolia, and Zimbabwe.

Philip also looked carefully at the footprints of meat-eating dinosaurs in the Peace River Canyon of Canada. The footprints showed that meat-eating dinosaurs may have traveled together.

By studying fossils, experts can create models like this life-size *Albertosaurus*.

Digging Deeper

Did some meat-eating dinosaurs spend time living and hunting together? Scientists still aren't sure. They can only make smart guesses based on the fossils they have found.

Other questions are still unanswered as well. Why did the albertosaurs at Brown's site die? What killed so many animals at one time? A big storm? A forest fire?

Philip Currie says that a paleontologist is like a detective. The mysterious death happened millions of years ago. No one saw it. Using clues, the scientist tries to tell what happened, how, and why. As long as there are fossils waiting to be found, the investigation continues.

Dig Deeper

How to Analyze the Text

Use these pages to learn about Conclusions and Point of View. Then read *The Albertosaurus Mystery* again to apply what you learned.

Conclusions

Informational texts like *The Albertosaurus Mystery* give many facts and details about a topic. You can use this text evidence along with your own ideas to make smart guesses about things the author does not say. This is called drawing **conclusions.**

Sometimes headings and signal words such as *so* and *therefore* are clues to help you draw conclusions.

Look back at pages 60 and 61. This is the beginning of the selection, but you can already tell that Philip Currie has a difficult job. There are details in the text, but also look at the section heading. Combine the text evidence with what you already know to draw conclusions.

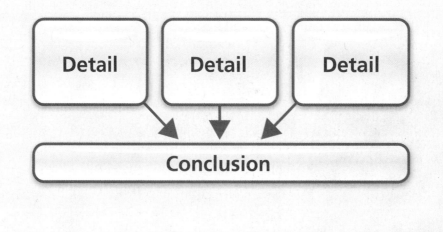

RI.3.1 ask and answer questions to demonstrate understanding, referring to the text; **RI.3.6** distinguish own point of view from that of the author

COMMON CORE

Point of View

An author has a **point of view** about his or her subject. The point of view is the author's opinion. Readers can also have a point of view about the author's subject. You may see a subject from the same point of view as the author. If so, you agree with what was written. Sometimes, you may have a different point of view.

For example, the author describes how hard Philip Currie worked to find Barnum Brown's bone bed. Her point of view is that Currie is determined. Is your point of view the same? If not, why?

Your Turn

Review the selection with a partner to prepare to discuss this question: *What can fossils tell us about the past?* As you discuss the question, take turns reviewing and explaining key ideas. Use text evidence to support your ideas.

Classroom Conversation

Continue your discussion of *The Albertosaurus Mystery.* Use text evidence to explain your answers to these questions:

1. How did Barnum Brown's old photo help Philip Currie find the bone bed?

2. Do you think that the fossils found so far have solved the mystery about meat-eating dinosaurs? Why or why not?

3. What text evidence might help answer the questions that Philip Currie still has?

WRITE ABOUT READING

Response Philip Currie found Barnum Brown's bone bed after the rest of the team had gone back to camp. What do you think might have happened if Philip had returned with the rest of his team? Would he have found the bone bed? Use text evidence to support your answer.

Writing Tip

As you write, check that you use the correct verb tense to tell about action that happened in the past.

RI.3.7 use information gained from illustrations and words to demonstrate understanding; **W.3.1a** introduce the topic, state an opinion, and create an organizational structure; **W.3.1b** provide reasons that support the opinion; **W.3.1d** provide a concluding statement or section; **SL.3.1a** come to discussions prepared/explicitly draw on preparation and other information about the topic; **SL.3.1d** explain own ideas and understanding in light of the discussion; **L.3.1e** form and use simple verb tenses

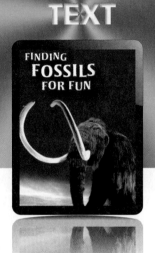

FINDING
FOSSILS
FOR FUN

| File | Edit | View | Favorites |

▸ FINDING FOSSILS FOR FUN

by ALICE CARY

Have you ever hunted for fossils? People often find them by accident. In 2007, a Florida high school student and her friends went to a creek to take photos for a school project. They saw lots of bones in the water. The girls were surprised! They had found the remains of an Ice Age mammoth.

Scientists began digging at the creek. Soon they were uncovering other animal skeletons.

A mammoth skeleton gives clues about how a mammoth looked.

Fossils

Fossils are evidence of ancient life. Sometimes dirt or sand covers leaves and bones. Layers of dirt and sand protect these remains from damage. The layers build up as time passes. After many years, the remains harden and become fossils.

You may find fossils buried near you! The chart gives you tips for hunting them.

Hunting Guide

Where to Look	What to Hunt	Tools	Searching Tips
layers of rock	eggs, nests	hammer and chisel	Work carefully so you don't miss anything.
layers of sand or mud	footprints, leaf impressions	notebook, pen, camera	Take notes to keep track of where each discovery was found.
deserts, canyons, cliffs, hills, and mountains	shells	plastic box or newspapers and rubber bands for carrying finds	Look for things that seem unusual or out of place.

Anyone Can Find Fossils!

You're never too young to find fossils. David Shiffler loved fierce dinosaurs. In 1995, when he was only three years old, David dug up a green rock. He called it a dinosaur egg.

David's father took the rock to a museum a few months later. David was right! He had found a piece of dinosaur egg! Scientists could prove it. The egg was about 150 million years old!

Hunt Fossils Safely

▶ Take an adult.
▶ Choose a safe location.
▶ Get permission to hunt before you start.
▶ Wear safety glasses.

COOL CLICKS!

Museums with Fossils

Fossils in the News

Fossil Finds

Compare Texts

Compare Methods Think about the fossil-hunting methods in *The Albertosaurus Mystery* and *Finding Fossils for Fun*. Discuss with a partner what the important ideas are in each selection. How are the ideas alike and different? Is there a method described in *Finding Fossils for Fun* that might help scientists find *Albertosaurus* bones?

Be a Fossil Hunter After reading about people who hunt for fossils, do you think you would like to be a fossil hunter? Write a paragraph explaining why or why not. Include evidence from the text to support your opinion.

Tell the Steps With a partner, discuss the steps you would follow on a fossil-hunting trip. Use evidence from *The Albertosaurus Mystery* and *Finding Fossils for Fun*. Be sure to tell the steps in order.

COMMON CORE **RI.3.1** ask and answer questions to demonstrate understanding, referring to the text; **RI.3.3** describe the relationship between a series of historical events/scientific ideas/steps in technical procedures; **RI.3.9** compare and contrast important points and details in texts on the same topic

L.3.1a explain the function of nouns, pronouns, verbs, adjectives, and adverbs; **L.3.1g** form and use comparative and superlative adjective and adverbs, and choose between them

Grammar

Adjectives That Compare Use **adjectives** to describe how people, places or things are alike or different. Some adjectives use different endings to compare nouns.

- Add -*er* to most adjectives to compare two people, places, or things.

    Tyrannosaurus rex was larger than *Albertosaurus*.

- Add -*est* to most adjectives to compare more than two people, places or things.

    Sam found the largest fossil that day.

Try This! **Copy each sentence. Fill in the blank with the correct form of the adjective in parentheses.**

1 The _____ dinosaur found is *Compsognathus*. (small)

2 It was just a bit _____ than a modern chicken. (large)

3 *Brachiosaurus* was _____ than a four-story building. (tall)

4 The _____ dinosaur found could run at about 40 miles an hour. (fast)

Adjectives add details about people, places, and things. When you write, use adjectives to give readers a good description. Use a comparative adjective, one with *-er*, when you compare two things. Use a superlative adjective, one with *-est*, when you compare more than two things.

Adjectives That Compare		
Adjective	**Compare Two**	**Compare More Than Two**
loud	loud**er**	loud**est**
great	great**er**	great**est**
warm	warm**er**	warm**est**

Connect Grammar to Writing

As you revise your opinion paragraph, look for adjectives. Make sure that when you compare nouns you use the correct form to match the number of objects.

COMMON CORE

Opinion Writing

✔ **Voice** The author of *The Albertosaurus Mystery* thinks fossil hunting is exciting. By sharing what really interests her, she gets her readers excited, too. In your **opinion paragraph**, add ideas and details that will support your opinion. Let readers know why you feel as you do.

Rick wrote his opinion of studying prehistoric people. Later, he added more details to support his opinion.

Writing Traits Checklist

✔ **Ideas**
Did I explain my ideas clearly?

✔ **Organization**
Did I begin by telling my opinion?

✔ **Word Choice**
Did I use exact adjectives?

✔ **Voice**
Are my supporting reasons and details right for my audience?

✔ **Sentence Fluency**
Do my sentences flow smoothly?

✔ **Conventions**
Did I punctuate my sentences correctly?

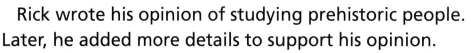

Revised Draft

I love learning about prehistoric people. The way scientists study them
like solving a mysterious puzzle.
is ~~interesting.~~ Prehistoric people left no
      ∧
books about their lives. They only left

objects that give clues. I am also

amazed by how they got along without

modern inventions. They lived in caves or
Imagine camping out for your whole life!
huts, even in freezing weather. ∧

Amazing People from the Past
by Rick Yoshida

I love learning about prehistoric people. The way scientists study them is like solving a mysterious puzzle. Prehistoric people left no books about their lives. They only left objects that give clues. I am also amazed by how they got along without modern inventions. They lived in caves or huts, even in freezing weather. Imagine camping out for your whole life! They got all their food by hunting or finding plants. Don't you wonder what kids did for fun? There are lots of great facts to learn about prehistoric people.

Lesson 18

TARGET VOCABULARY

pollen
store
clumps
passages
absorb
throughout
coverings
spines
tropical
dissolve

Vocabulary Reader

Context Cards

COMMON CORE **L.3.6** acquire and use conversational, general academic, and domain-specific words and phrases

Vocabulary in Context

1 pollen

This bee carries pollen from flower to flower, which helps seeds grow.

2 store

A baobab tree can store, or keep, lots of water in its trunk.

3 clumps

The flowers on some trees grow in clumps, or bunches.

4 passages

A leaf has small passages, or tubes, that allow water to spread all over.

Go Digital

▶ Study each Context Card.

▶ Make up a new context sentence using two Vocabulary words.

---

5 absorb

A plant's roots absorb water. They soak it up.

---

6 throughout

Sap passes throughout a tree. It travels to every part.

---

7 coverings

Different kinds of trees have different coverings, or outer layers.

---

8 spines

Many kinds of cacti are covered in sharp spines.

---

9 tropical

Some plants grow in warm, damp, tropical climates near the equator.

---

10 dissolve

If you add salt to water, it will dissolve, or mix, with the water.

A TREE IS GROWING
by ARTHUR DORROS
illustrated by S. D. SCHINDLER

Read and Comprehend

Go Digital

☑ TARGET SKILL

Text and Graphic Features As you read *A Tree Is Growing*, look for features that will help you understand the information. **Text features** such as labels, captions, and sidebars will give you more details about the main text. **Graphic features,** including pictures and diagrams, will show you what the text describes. Use a chart like the one below to list the features you find and their purposes.

Text or Graphic Feature	Page	Purpose

☑ TARGET STRATEGY

Question As you read, ask yourself **questions** to make sure that you understand the information. Look for evidence in the words, sidebars, pictures, labels, and diagrams.

COMMON CORE

RI.3.1 ask and answer questions to demonstrate understanding, referring to the text; **RI.3.5** use text features and search tools to locate information; **RI.3.7** use information gained from illustrations and words to demonstrate understanding

Trees

Trees are a great natural resource. Apart from their beauty, trees provide shade and food. Trees protect people from windstorms and floods. People use the wood from trees to build houses and to keep their homes warm, as well as to make useful things such as furniture, paper, and pencils. As a resource, trees are especially valuable because they are renewable. This means that new trees can be planted to replace the trees that people use.

In *A Tree Is Growing*, you will read about the science of how trees grow. You may find some fascinating facts!

ANCHOR TEXT

A TREE IS GROWING

by ARTHUR DORROS
Illustrated by S. D. SCHINDLER

✅ TARGET SKILL

Text and Graphic Features
As you read, use text features and graphic features to help you understand the information.

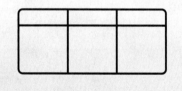

✅ GENRE

Informational text gives you information about a topic. As you read, look for:

▶ photographs and captions
▶ graphics, such as diagrams, that help explain the topic
▶ text structure, or the ways the ideas and information are organized

 RI.3.5 use text features and search tools to locate information; **RI.3.7** use information gained from illustrations and words to demonstrate understanding; **RI.3.10** read and comprehend informational texts

MEET THE AUTHOR

Arthur Dorros

Arthur Dorros loves trees. When he was five, he planted a maple seedling. The tree grew taller than a two-story house! The author believes that everyone has stories to tell. He encourages children all over the country to write.

MEET THE ILLUSTRATOR

S. D. Schindler

When S. D. Schindler was just four years old, he won a red wagon in a coloring contest. S. D. Schindler loves nature as much as he loves art. He used plants and animals from the woods near his home as models for the illustrations in *A Tree Is Growing*.

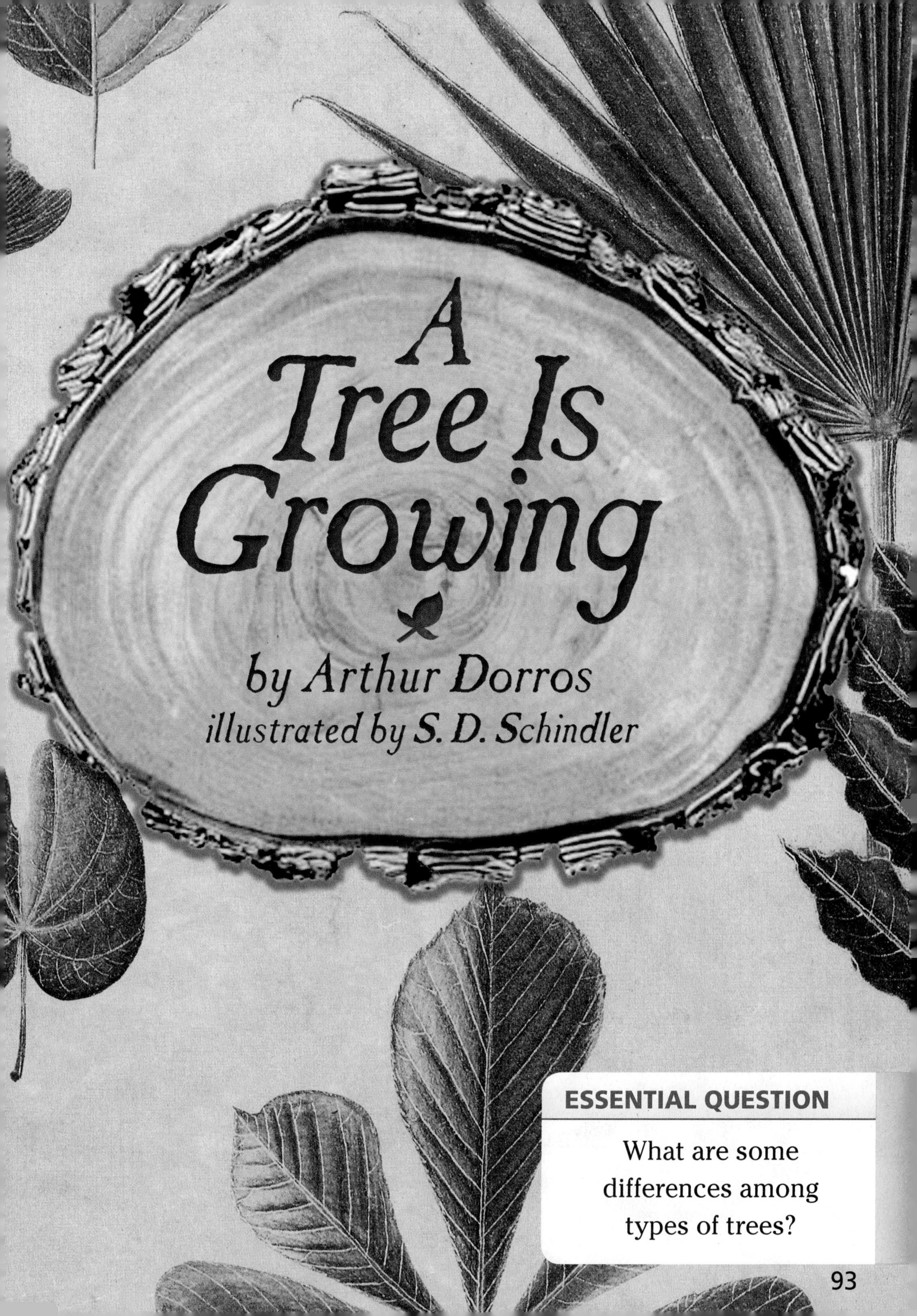

A Tree Is Growing

by Arthur Dorros

illustrated by S. D. Schindler

ESSENTIAL QUESTION

What are some differences among types of trees?

A giant tree may look as if it has always been big. But even the biggest tree keeps growing and changing.

In the spring you can see that a tree is growing as you watch buds on the branches unfold into leaves.

Bristlecone pines
are the oldest
known living trees
on earth. Some
have been growing
for five thousand
years—since before
the pyramids in
Egypt were built.

95

White oak

Palm

Gingko

Leaves can be skinny needles or big heart shapes. Whatever shape or size a leaf is, it makes food for the tree.

A kind of sugar is made in the leaves. Trees use the sugar as food.

Breadfruit tree

Empress tree

White pine

Red maple

*If you rub a
sassafras leaf,
the sap smells spicy.*

The sugary water made in the leaves is mixed with other tree juices called sap. The food in the sap is carried throughout the tree. Where a branch breaks or where bark is cut, sap oozes out of a tree. The strong smells of some saps can keep insects from eating the trees they live on.

*Maple syrup is the
boiled sap of sugar
maple trees.*

97

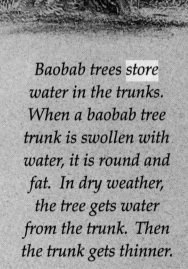

Moth
caterpillar

Baobab trees store water in the trunks. When a baobab tree trunk is swollen with water, it is round and fat. In dry weather, the tree gets water from the trunk. Then the trunk gets thinner.

Water

A tree needs sunlight, air, soil, and water to grow.

Water travels through passages in the trunk and branches up to the leaves. The water moves up the trunk as if it is being sucked through a straw.

Sugary sap made in the leaves travels down other passages in the trunk, taking food to different parts of the tree.

A few kinds of trees drop roots from branches into the soil to gather water. Banyan tree roots grow into columns all around the tree.

Growing roots are strong. A root can lift a sidewalk or split a rock as it grows. By splitting the rock, it helps make soil.

White oak

Earthworms

Beetle grub

The roots of a tree grow into the ground and hold the tree in place. Roots are like pipelines. They absorb water and carry it into the tree.

A tree's roots spread out far underground. They usually grow out a little farther than the tree's branches.

Trees need minerals to grow. Minerals are tiny particles that are found in the soil. Salt is one kind of mineral. Like salt, other minerals dissolve in water. They are mixed in with the water that roots absorb and are carried throughout the tree.

Mushrooms growing among the roots of a tree can help it get minerals. And the mushrooms and plants growing near a tree get water brought by the tree's roots.

Bicolored boletus mushrooms

Flicker

Bark is the skin of a tree. The outer layer of bark protects the tree. When an oak tree is young, the bark is as smooth as a baby's skin. As the tree grows older, the bark becomes rough and cracked.

Polyphemus
moth

Looking at the bark
of a tree can help
you know what
kind of tree it is.

The cork used for
bulletin boards is
the peeled-off
outer bark of a
cork oak tree.

Honey locust bark
has spines to help
protect the tree.

In cool climates, cambium only grows in spring and summer. Count growth rings to see how old a tree was when it died. An old fir tree can have over a thousand rings, one for each year it lived.

In tropical rain forest trees, the cambium grows all year and there are no rings. It is hard to tell the ages of those trees.

Growth rings

Snail

Phloem

Cambium

Xylem

ANALYZE THE TEXT

Text and Graphic Features How do the captions, labels, and diagrams help you understand the selection?

Underwing moth

The bark you can touch and see is not growing anymore. Underneath it is a layer of growing bark, called *cambium*. Each year's cambium growth is a ring in the wood of a tree. As trees add new cambium, the trees become bigger around.

Next to the cambium are two layers called *xylem* and *phloem*. Water from the roots moves through the xylem, and sap from the leaves moves through the phloem.

Trees grow bigger around, and they grow taller. As a tree grows, lower branches may fall off, making the trunk look longer. But the branches do not move upward on the trunk. A tree grows taller only at the top, as the tips of the top branches grow upward.

If you find a mark on a tree trunk today, that mark would stay at the same height for as long as the tree lives.

10 years   20 years   30 years

Wild turkey

50 years   200 years

Sequoias are some of the tallest trees in the world—over three hundred feet tall.

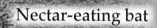

Nectar-eating bat

Catkins

Calabash tree

Purple finch
(male)

Saucer
magnolia

Birds, insects, and even bats are attracted to flowers to drink their sweet juices. When they brush the flowers, the animals get a powder called pollen on them. The animals carry the pollen to other flowers. When the pollen mixes with certain parts of the flowers, seeds grow. Wind also helps pollinate flowers.

108

In the spring, you can smell tree flowers. Tree flowers are found in many shapes and colors, and have many different smells. Parts of the flowers grow to become seeds. Oak trees have dangling clumps of flowers called catkins that help make acorns, the seeds of an oak tree.

Honey bee

Wild cherry

Purple finch (female)

ANALYZE THE TEXT

Domain-Specific Vocabulary
What words can you find on these two pages that are related to life science? What do they mean?

Sugar maple

An oak tree can drop more than fifty thousand acorns in one year. Only a few of them grow into oak trees. Most are eaten, are crushed, rot, or land in a place where they cannot take root.

Acorns can be carried away and dropped or buried by animals to grow in new places. Other kinds of seeds blow in the wind or float on water.

Sugar maple seed

Acorns

Gray
squirrel

Different kinds of trees
make seeds with
different coverings.
Nuts, cones, and fruits
all have seeds inside.

Mountain
pine cone

Brazil nut

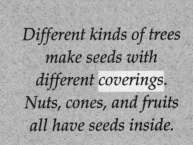

Cherry

Coconuts are seeds of
a palm tree. A coconut
can float across the
ocean and sprout on a
sandy beach.

Autumn is a great time to collect leaves. Each tree has its own special color.

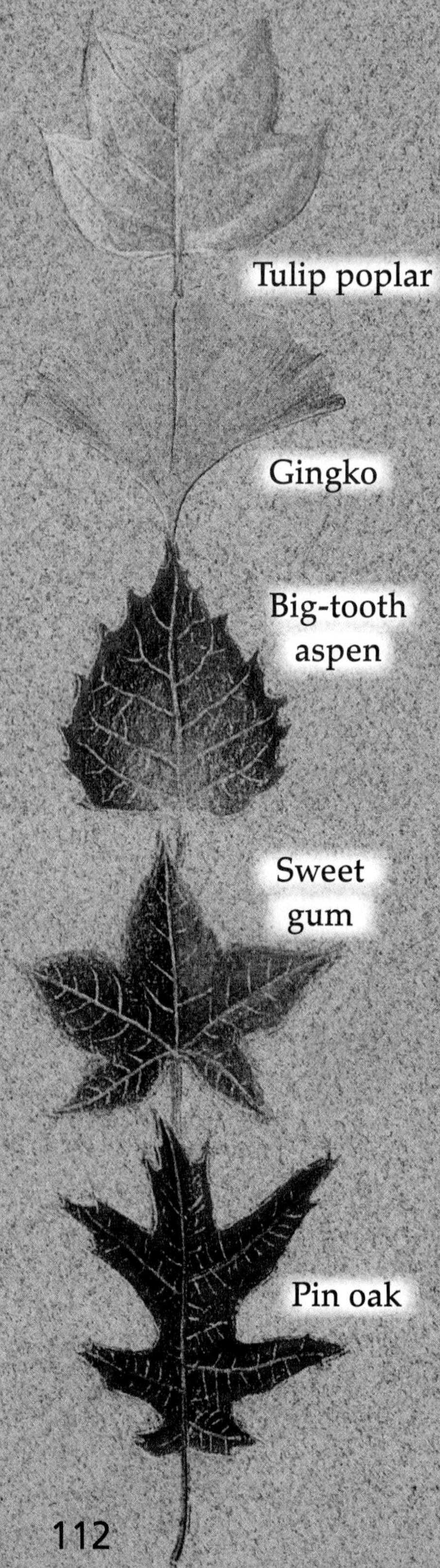
Tulip poplar
Gingko
Big-tooth aspen
Sweet gum
Pin oak

In cool climates, trees stop growing in autumn. The leaves of many trees stop making sugary food for the tree, and they lose their green color. Then you can see the red, brown, yellow, and orange colors that are also in the leaves.

Pine trees and some other trees have needles or leaves that do not change color in autumn.

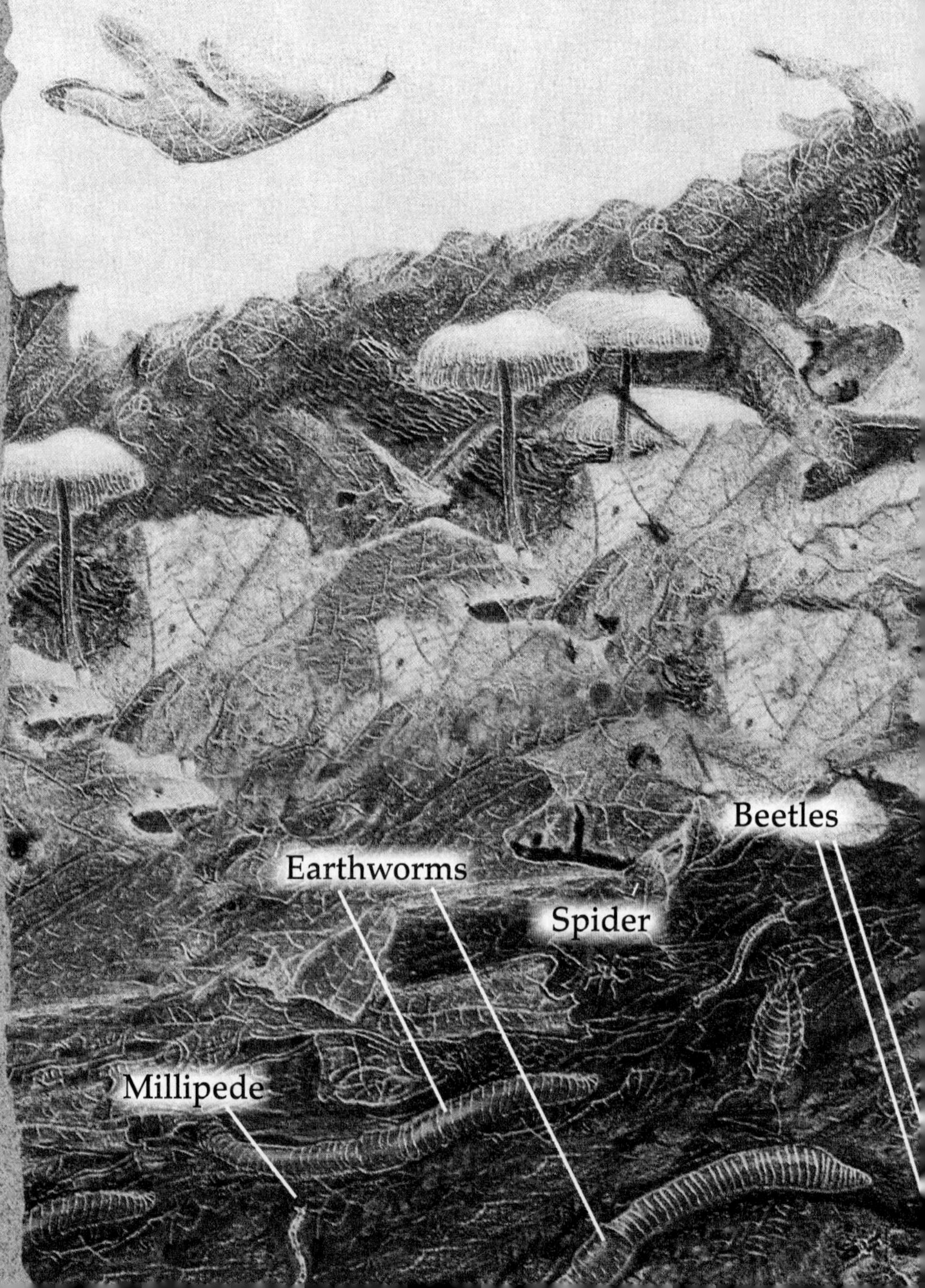
Beetles
Earthworms
Spider
Millipede

Mole

When leaves fall to the ground, insects and worms eat them. The chewed and eaten bits of leaves make the soil better for growing trees and other plants.

White oak

White oak

Horse chestnut

114

Trees rest in the cold of winter, and their branches are bare. They may look as if they are dead. But look closely and you can see small buds that will become leaves and flowers in the spring.

In the spring, listen to the wind rustling the leaves. The trees are growing again.

A TREE IS GROWING

Dig Deeper

How to Analyze the Text
Use these pages to learn about Text and Graphic Features and Domain-Specific Vocabulary. Then read *A Tree Is Growing* again to apply what you learned.

Text and Graphic Features

Informational text, such as *A Tree Is Growing*, gives facts and details about a topic. Besides the main text, readers can find information in other ways. Sidebars are a **text feature** next to the main text. A sidebar gives more details about a part of the main text and may also have pictures. **Graphic features** include pictures and diagrams that help to explain the main text. Labels identify parts of pictures and diagrams or show how something works.

Look back at page 96 in *A Tree Is Growing*. Here, labeled pictures show different kinds of leaves. On page 99, a diagram shows how water travels up a tree.

Use a chart like the one below to help you identify each feature and its purpose.

Text or Graphic Feature	Page	Purpose

RI.3.4 determine the meaning of general academic and domain-specific words and phrases; **RI.3.5** use text features and search tools to locate information; **RI.3.7** use information gained from illustrations and words to demonstrate understanding; **L.3.4a** use sentence-level context as a clue to the meaning of a word or phrase; **L.3.6** acquire and use conversational, general academic, and domain-specific words and phrases

COMMON CORE

Go Digital

Domain-Specific Vocabulary

A Tree Is Growing provides scientific information about how trees grow. The selection includes special words that are a part of the **domain,** or subject, of science. Use context clues to figure out what a science word means.

In the sidebar on page 104 is the word *cambium.* The text on page 105 says that cambium is "a layer of growing bark." The text also explains the words *xylem* and *phloem.*

Your Turn

Turn and Talk Review the text with a partner to prepare to discuss this question: *What are some differences among types of trees?* As you discuss, take turns reviewing and explaining the key ideas in your discussion. Use text evidence to support your ideas.

Classroom Conversation

Continue your discussion of *A Tree Is Growing* by using text evidence to explain your answers to these questions:

1 Why is it difficult to tell the age of a tree in the tropical rain forest?

2 Why do some trees look dead in the winter? What is really happening to these trees?

3 What kinds of trees grow where you live? What do you know about those trees?

WRITE ABOUT READING

Response Think about what you learned in *A Tree Is Growing.* How do you feel about trees now? Use text evidence and your own ideas to write a poem about trees. Share your poem by reading it to a partner.

Writing Tip

Descriptive words will help your readers picture what you write about. Think of colorful adjectives and verbs to describe your trees.

RI.3.1 ask and answer questions to demonstrate understanding, referring to the text; **RI.3.7** use information gained from illustrations and words to demonstrate understanding; **W.3.10** write routinely over extended time frames or short time frames; **SL.3.1a** come to discussions prepared/explicitly draw on preparation and other information about the topic; **SL.3.1d** explain own ideas and understanding in light of the discussion; **L.3.3a** choose words and phrases for effect

POETRY

✓ GENRE

Poetry uses the sound and rhythm of words to show images and express feelings.

✓ TEXT FOCUS

A poem can be broken into **stanzas,** or groups of lines. Often, each stanza follows the same rhyming pattern.

COMMON CORE **RL.3.5** refer to parts of stories, dramas, and poems/describe how each part builds on earlier sections; **RL.3.10** read and comprehend literature

Stopping by Woods on a Snowy Evening

Whose woods these are I think I know.
His house is in the village though;
He will not see me stopping here
To watch his woods fill up with snow.

My little horse must think it queer
To stop without a farmhouse near
Between the woods and frozen lake
The darkest evening of the year.

He gives his harness bells a shake
To ask if there is some mistake.
The only other sound's the sweep
Of easy wind and downy flake.

The woods are lovely, dark and deep,
But I have promises to keep,
And miles to go before I sleep,
And miles to go before I sleep.

by Robert Frost

Compare Texts

Compare Seasons Think about how the woods in "Stopping by Woods on a Snowy Evening" look to the poet. Use evidence from *A Tree Is Growing* to think about how those trees would look during the spring. Write a list to compare and contrast the trees in winter and spring. Then write a paragraph.

Discuss Living Things In what ways are you like a tree? In what ways are you different? Work in a small group. Take turns telling how you are like a tree and how you are different.

Talk About Poems With a partner, compare and contrast "Stopping by Woods on a Snowy Evening" and another poem, such as "A Bat Is Born" from Lesson 6. In your discussion, use poetry terms such as *stanza* and *rhyme*. If possible, record yourself reading each poem.

COMMON CORE **RL 3.5** refer to parts of stories, dramas, and poems/describe how each part builds on earlier sections; **RI.3.9** compare and contrast important points and details in texts on the same topic; **SL.3.1d** explain own ideas and understanding in light of the discussion; **SL.3.5** create recordings of stories or poems that demonstrate fluid reading at an understanding pace/add visual displays

123

Grammar

Using the Verb *be* and Helping Verbs The verbs *am*, *is*, *was*, *are*, and *were* are forms of the verb *be*. They do not show action. They tell what someone or something is or was.

Subject	Present Tense	Past Tense
I	am	was
you	are	were
he, she, it	is	was
singular noun (*tree*)	is	was
plural noun (*trees*), we, they	are	were

Sometimes the words *has* and *have* help other verbs to show past time. *Has* and *have* are called **helping verbs.**

Subject	Helping Verb
he, she, it	He has watched the trees grow.
I, you, we, they	They have grown very tall.

Try This! **Write each sentence correctly using the verb form that best completes each sentence.**

1. I (is, am) a great tree climber.

2. The girls (has, have) picked apples.

3. They (was, were) at the orchard yesterday.

When two sentences have the same predicate, you can put the sentences together. Join the two subjects and use the word *and* between them. You may have to change the forms of the verbs *be* and *have* to go with their subjects.

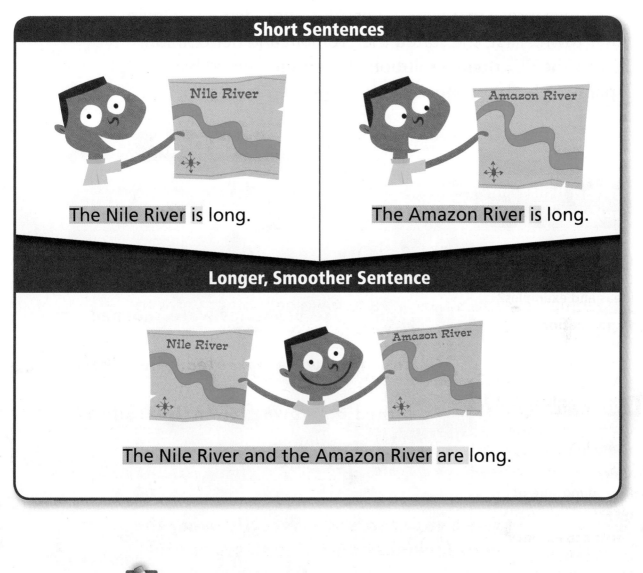

Short Sentences

The Nile River is long.

The Amazon River is long.

Longer, Smoother Sentence

The Nile River and the Amazon River are long.

Connect Grammar to Writing

As you revise your problem-and-solution paragraph, try to combine subjects to make longer sentences. Make sure that the verb form goes with the subject.

COMMON CORE **W.3.1a** introduce the topic, state an opinion, and create an organizational structure; **W.3.1b** provide reasons that support the opinion; **W.3.1c** use linking words and phrases to connect opinion and reasons; **W.3.1d** provide a concluding statement or section; **L.3.3a** choose words and phrases for effect

Opinion Writing

✔ **Word Choice** A **problem-and-solution paragraph** presents a problem and ideas about how to solve it. Using clear, exact words will help readers understand how you feel about a problem and what you would do to fix it.

Tanya wrote to a newspaper about her idea for helping her town. First, she stated the problem and her opinion. Then she described a solution. When she revised her paragraph, she changed words to make her ideas clearer.

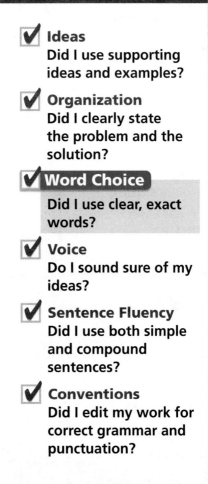

Writing Traits Checklist

✔ **Ideas**
Did I use supporting ideas and examples?

✔ **Organization**
Did I clearly state the problem and the solution?

✔ **Word Choice**
Did I use clear, exact words?

✔ **Voice**
Do I sound sure of my ideas?

✔ **Sentence Fluency**
Did I use both simple and compound sentences?

✔ **Conventions**
Did I edit my work for correct grammar and punctuation?

Revised Draft

Since the ~~big~~ historic snowstorm last fall, our town park has looked sad and bare. Many huge branches were snapped off, and trees were uprooted. ~~The storm~~ Twenty inches of snow turned our town from a Tree City to a No-Tree City.

Help Our Tree City

by Tanya Petrov

Since the historic snowstorm last fall, our town park has looked sad and bare. Many huge branches were snapped off, and trees were uprooted. Twenty inches of snow turned our town from a Tree City to a No-Tree City. Visitors pass the park when they come here. As it is now, the park looks like we don't care about trees. I believe our town can be a Tree City again. Arbor Day is the last Friday in April. On that day, our city can have a "Plant a Tree" event. I have talked to the teachers and students in my school. They are ready to help plan the event and plant the trees. Visitors will see all the new trees and know that our town loves trees.

Reading as a Writer

Why did Tanya replace "the storm" with "twenty inches of snow"? Where can you add more exact words in your paragraph?

I added some exact words to make my ideas more detailed and clear.

Vocabulary in Context

☑ **TARGET VOCABULARY**

scolding
greedily
ignores
hesitation
burden
glancing
base
console
drowsy
heroic

Vocabulary Reader

Context Cards

L.3.6 acquire and use conversational, general academic, and domain-specific words and phrases

128

1 scolding
This lion is scolding its cubs after they misbehaved.

2 greedily
The chipmunk eats greedily and does not share with others.

3 ignores
The fawn ignores its mother because it is paying attention to something far away.

4 hesitation
The bear shows hesitation as the hikers walk by.

Go Digital

▶ Study each Context Card.

▶ Use Vocabulary words to tell a story about two or more pictures.

5 burden

The travelers have placed a heavy burden, or load, on the yak.

6 glancing

The boy is glancing, or looking quickly, at something outside the window.

7 base

Water flows near the base, or bottom, of the mountain known as El Capitan.

8 console

The girl's mother tries to console her after she fell and hurt herself.

9 drowsy

After hunting, the fox became drowsy and fell asleep in its den.

10 heroic

The heroic campers fought the wildfire until help arrived.

Read and Comprehend

✓ **TARGET SKILL**

Story Structure Some parts of plays are just like other stories. As you read the play *Two Bear Cubs*, look for the setting and the main characters. Identify the problem that the characters face and how they solve it.

Unlike other stories, plays are organized by **scenes** that help to break up a performance on stage. Note how the plot events in each scene lead to the events in the next scene. Use a story map like this one to record text evidence about the **setting, characters,** and **plot.**

Setting	Characters
Plot	
Scene 1 Scene 2 Scene 3	

✓ **TARGET STRATEGY**

Summarize Identify the main action that occurs in each scene of *Two Bear Cubs*. Then combine these events to **summarize,** or retell briefly, the plot of the play.

 COMMON CORE **RL.3.2** recount stories and determine the message, lesson, or moral; **RL.3.5** refer to parts of stories, dramas, and poems/describe how each part builds on earlier sections

Social Relationships

The huge rock El Capitan rises out of the beautiful Yosemite Valley of California. The Miwok are American Indians whose ancestors lived in the valley for hundreds of years. For centuries, the Miwok have told a myth that explains how the rock first came to be.

Yet the myth tells more than that. It shows that the Miwok believed it was important for a community to come together to help each other in times of trouble. In *Two Bear Cubs*, you'll read the Miwok myth as a play. You'll see how the animals try to help when two bear cubs and their mother are in need.

ANCHOR TEXT

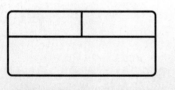

✓ TARGET SKILL

Story Structure Identify the setting, characters, and plot of the play as you read. Note how the action in each scene, or part of the play, leads to the next scene.

✓ GENRE

A **play** is a story that can be performed for an audience. As you read, look for:
- ▶ headings that tell you where the scenes begin
- ▶ dialogue, or the words of the characters
- ▶ stage directions

COMMON CORE **RL.3.2** recount stories and determine the message, lesson, or moral; **RL.3.5** refer to parts of stories, dramas, and poems/describe how each part builds on earlier sections; **RL.3.10** read and comprehend literature

MEET THE PLAYWRIGHT

Robert D. San Souci

Most of Robert D. San Souci's ideas for books come from reading and researching. He is fascinated by folktales from around the world. His books are retellings of these stories.

MEET THE ILLUSTRATOR

Tracy Walker

Tracy Walker likes to study the natural forms that are around her, such as trees, plants, and flowers. She likes the designs of nature and uses these designs to inspire her art.

Two Bear Cubs

from a Miwok myth
adapted by Robert D. San Souci
illustrated by Tracy Walker

Characters:

STORYTELLER
MOTHER GRIZZLY
OLDER BROTHER
YOUNGER BROTHER
HAWK
FOX
BADGER
MOTHER DEER
2 FAWNS
MOUNTAIN LION
MOUSE
MEASURING WORM (TU-TOK-A-NA)

ESSENTIAL QUESTION

How do members of
a community help
each other?

133

PROLOGUE

STORYTELLER: (*Enters from stage left*) Many snows have come and gone since this story was first told. My people, the Miwok, live in California—some in what is now called Yosemite Valley. We tell stories of the old days, when animal people lived in the valley. One story begins with MOTHER GRIZZLY going to the river to catch fish for herself and her cubs (*Exits*).

SCENE 1

SETTING: *A forest and mountain, stage left; open sky dotted with clouds, stage right. Blue cloth or painted cardboard across the front of the stage suggests a river.*

(MOTHER GRIZZLY *enters from stage left, holding a fish basket, and stands on the riverbank. Her cubs,* YOUNGER BROTHER *and* OLDER BROTHER *enter and begin to play in the "water."*)

OLDER BROTHER (*Laughing and splashing*): Don't be afraid of a little water, Younger Brother!

YOUNGER BROTHER (*Splashing back*): I'm not, Older Brother!

MOTHER GRIZZLY (*Scolding*): Children! Stop scaring away the fish, or we will have nothing to eat. Out of the water, now! (*They obey but manage a last splash or two.*) I want you to gather berries— but stay close and do not go downriver. Strange things happen there.

(MOTHER GRIZZLY *moves to stage left; the* CUBS *move to stage right, while playing and pushing each other. A berry bush appears.*)

OLDER BROTHER: Look at these berries. (*He picks and eats them greedily.*) They are so sweet. Taste them!

YOUNGER BROTHER: We should take them back to Mother. (*When* OLDER BROTHER *ignores him, the younger cub begins eating berries, too. Suddenly, he rubs his stomach.*) I have eaten too many!

OLDER BROTHER: We will bring some back later. Oh, I am full, too. (*Pointing—*) Let's see what is downriver.

YOUNGER BROTHER (*Worried*): We are not supposed to go there.

OLDER BROTHER (*Taunting, starts off*): I see only the river and trees and stones. What is there to fear?

(*After a moment's hesitation,* YOUNGER BROTHER *follows.*)

YOUNGER BROTHER (*Rubbing his eyes*): I'm tired. The hot sun and my full belly make me want to sleep.

OLDER BROTHER (*Yawning*): A nap would be good.

(*A raised platform, decorated to look like a rock, slides into view.*)

YOUNGER BROTHER (*Pointing*): See that big, flat rock. It looks so warm. Let's rest there. (*The* CUBS *lie down side-by-side, stretch, and fall asleep.*)

STORYTELLER (*Entering, stage left*): The cubs fell asleep on the stone. But the stone was the seed of a mountain. As they slept, the stone grew bigger and bigger, higher and higher. (*His hand spiraling upward suggests the growing mountain.*) It carried them so high that only Hawk saw them as he flew by (*Pauses*) . . .

(**HAWK** *enters, stage right, waving his arms like wings. He "flies" past the rock, looks at the sleeping* **CUBS**, *and then "flies" back offstage the way he came.*)

STORYTELLER (*Continuing*): . . . Meanwhile, Mother Grizzly wondered what had become of her cubs (*Exits stage left*).

SCENE 2

(FOX *and* BADGER *are onstage, leaning cedar planks against a tent-shaped frame of poles.*)

MOTHER GRIZZLY (*Enters, stage left, calling*): Older Brother! Younger Brother!

(MOTHER GRIZZLY *sees* FOX *and* BADGER.) Fox! Badger! Have you seen my cubs?

FOX: No. I have been helping Badger build a new home.

BADGER: Neither of us has seen them. We will help you look for them.

(FOX, BADGER, *and* MOTHER GRIZZLY *search to the right.* MOTHER DEER *and* FAWNS *enter, stage left, and seat themselves, grinding acorns.* FOX, BADGER, *and* MOTHER GRIZZLY *return to stage left and discover* MOTHER DEER *and her two* FAWNS.)

MOTHER GRIZZLY: Mother Deer, my little ones are missing. Have you seen them?

MOTHER DEER: They have not come by while my children and I were grinding acorns. But we will help you find them.

(MOTHER DEER *and* FAWNS *rise and join the others as they move, to stage right, and then back again, to left. They meet* MOUNTAIN LION, *carrying a load of firewood.*)

ANALYZE THE TEXT

Story Structure How can you tell that this is a new scene? How does it build on what happens in Scene 1?

MOTHER GRIZZLY: Mountain Lion, we are looking for my lost cubs.

MOUNTAIN LION (*Sets her burden down*): I will help you find them.

(ALL *move to stage right, while* MOUSE *enters from left and sits.* MOUSE *is weaving a basket. The group at stage right moves left and meets* MOUSE.)

MOTHER GRIZZLY: Mouse, have you seen my cubs? We have searched everywhere for them. We have looked in hollow logs and caves and in the berry patch and the honey tree.

MOUSE (*Rising*): No, but I will help you. Perhaps they went downriver.

MOTHER GRIZZLY: I warned them not to go there.

MOTHER DEER (*Patting* MOTHER GRIZZLY's *shoulder and glancing at her own* FAWNS): Sometimes our little ones do not listen very well. I agree that we should look downriver.

(*The* ANIMALS *onstage move slowly toward the "mountain."*)

Fox (*Stopping, pointing*): Look, everyone. There is a mountain where there was only a stone before.

(ALL *slowly raise their heads as they scan the mountain from base to summit. As they do,* HAWK *enters as before, flapping his wings.*)

MOTHER GRIZZLY: I see Hawk. (*Cups paws around her mouth and shouts "up" to* HAWK—) Hawk! Have you seen my lost cubs?

HAWK (*Calling "down"*): They are asleep on this strange new mountain.

MOTHER GRIZZLY (*Calling "up"*): Please fly to my children, wake them, and help them find their way down.

(HAWK *pantomimes flying toward* CUBS *and being blown back by mountain winds. After several tries, he speaks to those "below."*)

HAWK (*Calling "down"*): The wind will not let me reach your little ones. Someone will have to climb up and rescue them.

STORYTELLER (*Enters, stage left*): One by one, the animals tried to reach the cubs. (ANIMALS *pantomime their attempts as* STORYTELLER *speaks*). Mother Grizzly tried several times but always tumbled back. Mouse jumped from stone to stone but quickly got scared and jumped back down. Badger climbed a bit higher. Mother Deer, a little bit higher. Fox did even better. But none succeeded. Even Mountain Lion failed.

(*When* MOTHER GRIZZLY *sees this, she begins to weep. The other creatures gather around to* console *her. Unnoticed by them,* MEASURING WORM *enters.*)

MOTHER GRIZZLY (*Sadly*): Mountain Lion, you are the best climber and were my best hope. There is no one now who can save my cubs.

MEASURING WORM: I will try.

(*The other animals turn and stare at him, and then* ALL *except* MOTHER GRIZZLY *begin to laugh.*)

MOUNTAIN LION: Foolish Measuring Worm! Do you think you can do what the rest of us have failed to do?

MOUSE (*Meanly*): *Tu-tok-a-na!* Your name is longer than you are.

STORYTELLER (*Appearing stage left*): My people call Measuring Worm *Tu-tok-a-na*, which means "Little Curl-Stretch." He moves by stretching—*tu*—then curling—*tok*—the way a caterpillar moves.

MOTHER GRIZZLY (*Drying her eyes*): I welcome your help.

(*MEASURING WORM begins to climb, all the while crying, "Tu-tok!" The other ANIMALS sit, staring at the mountain, watching as the WORM stretches and curls in a climbing motion.*)

MEASURING WORM (*Loudly*): *Tu-tok! Tu-tok!*

SCENE 3

STORYTELLER: In time Measuring Worm climbed even higher than Mountain Lion. He climbed so high that the animals below could no longer see or hear him. Sometimes he would grow afraid and stop when he saw how high he had climbed and how much higher he had to go. Then he thought about poor Mother Grizzly so worried at the bottom of the mountain. He thought about the cubs in danger at the top. Then he found his courage again and continued to climb, all the while crying—

MEASURING WORM: *Tu-tok! Tu-tok! Tu-tok!*

(STORYTELLER *exits as* MEASURING WORM *finally crawls onto the rock. He bends over the two sleeping* CUBS *and calls—*)

MEASURING WORM: Wake up!

(*The* CUBS *are drowsy as they wake and stretch and yawn.*)

OLDER BROTHER (*Crawls and looks over the side of the "rock"*): Younger Brother! Something terrible has happened. Look how high we are.

YOUNGER BROTHER (*Also on his knees, peers down*): We are trapped here. We will never get back to our mother.

(*The* CUBS *begin to cry. They have forgotten* MEASURING WORM.)

MEASURING WORM (*Comforting the* CUBS): Do not be afraid. I have come to guide you safely down the mountain. Just follow me, and do as I say. We will follow the safe path that brought me here.

OLDER BROTHER: I am afraid I will fall.

YOUNGER BROTHER: I am scared, too.

MEASURING WORM (*Gently*): Surely Mother Grizzly's children are not so afraid, for she is the bravest creature in the valley.

OLDER BROTHER (*Puffing out his chest, and beating it with his paw*): We are grizzlies. We are brave.

YOUNGER BROTHER (*Doing same*): We will follow you.

(*They pantomime following a safe path in single file, with* MEASURING WORM *leading,* OLDER BROTHER *following, and* YOUNGER BROTHER *behind. Below,* FOX *suddenly spots something, stands up, and peers more closely.*)

147

Fox (*Excitedly, pointing to a spot about halfway up the mountain*): Mother Grizzly. Look! Measuring Worm is guiding your cubs down the mountain.

(*All* ANIMALS *look where* Fox *is pointing.*)

MOTHER GRIZZLY (*Joyful, fearful*): Be careful, my children!

MOTHER DEER (*Reassuring her friend*): Trust Measuring Worm. He has brought them safely this far. He will not fail you now.

(*The* ANIMALS *continue to watch. They slowly lower their gaze to follow the climbers as they come down the mountain. At last the* CUBS *and* MEASURING WORM *make a final leap from the "mountain" to the "ground." The* CUBS *run to their mother.* MOTHER GRIZZLY *gives them a big hug. Then she pushes them away and shakes her finger at them.*)

MOTHER GRIZZLY (*Scolding*): Both of you have been very naughty! Look at the trouble and worry you have caused us all. You did not listen to me and went where you were not supposed to go!

OLDER BROTHER (*Hanging head*): I'm sorry. I won't do it again.

YOUNGER BROTHER (*Starting to cry*): I will never disobey you again.

ANALYZE THE TEXT

Story Message Which character's actions give an example for readers to follow? What does this tell you about the story's message?

MOTHER GRIZZLY (*Gathering them up in her arms again*): Be sure that you remember what happened today. But do not cry, little ones. It has all ended well, thanks to the help and courage of Measuring Worm.

149

(*The* ANIMALS *gather around* MEASURING WORM *and congratulate him.*)

STORYTELLER (*Enters, stage left*): Then all the animals decided to call the new mountain *Tu-tok-a-nu-la*, which means "Measuring Worm Stone." This was to honor the heroic worm who did what no other creature could do—he saved the two bear cubs. The mountain held this name for many years, until newcomers named the mountain El Capitan. We Miwok still call the mountain *Tu-tok-a-nu-la* to this day.

THE END

Dig Deeper

How to Analyze the Text

Use these pages to learn about Story Structure and Story Message. Then read *Two Bear Cubs* again to apply what you learned.

Story Structure

A myth, such as *Two Bear Cubs*, tells a story. Like all stories, it has a **setting** where the story takes place. It has **characters** who are the animals in the story. It also has a **plot,** which tells the order of events in which characters solve a problem.

Two Bear Cubs is written as a play, so the plot is divided into **scenes** instead of chapters. Headings tell you where each new scene begins. The action in each scene builds on the action that happened in the previous scene. The characters are listed on page 133. In the prologue on page 134, the storyteller describes the setting.

Setting	Characters
Plot	
Scene 1	
Scene 2	
Scene 3	

RL.3.2 recount stories and determine the message, lesson or moral; **RL.3.5** refer to parts of stories, dramas, and poems/describe how each part builds on earlier sections

Story Message

Traditional stories like *Two Bear Cubs* have a message. The **message** says something important about life or how to live.

The message is not directly stated. Instead, readers must look at how the characters act and what happens in the story. These details, or text evidence, can help readers answer the questions, "What can I learn about life from this story? What is the story's message?"

Your Turn

Turn and Talk Review *Two Bear Cubs* with a partner to prepare to discuss this question: *How do members of a community help each other?* As you discuss, take turns reviewing and explaining the key ideas in your discussion. Include evidence from the text to support your ideas.

Classroom Conversation

Continue your discussion by using text evidence to explain your answers to these questions:

1. How do the animals first react when Measuring Worm says he will find the cubs? Why?

2. How does Measuring Worm persuade the cubs to follow him down the mountain?

3. What can you learn about Miwok beliefs and values from this story?

WRITE ABOUT READING

Response Measuring Worm helps bring the cubs back safely to Mother Grizzly. What qualities did he show when helping the cubs? Use text evidence to write a character description of Measuring Worm.

Writing Tip

Use precise words when describing the qualities of Measuring Worm. Give an example of each quality from the text.

Go Digital

COMMON CORE

RL.3.1 ask and answer questions to demonstrate understanding, referring to the text; **RL.3.3** describe characters and explain how their actions contribute to the sequence of events; **RL.3.5** refer to parts of stories, dramas, and poems/describe how each part builds on earlier sections; **W.3.10** write routinely over extended time frames or short time frames; **SL.3.1d** explain own ideas and understanding in light of the discussion

Whose Land Is It?
by Ellen Gold

☑ GENRE

Informational text gives factual information about a topic. This is a newspaper feature article.

☑ TEXT FOCUS

Photographs show true pictures of important text details. **Captions** tell more about these photos.

RI.3.7 use information gained from illustrations and words to demonstrate understanding; **RI.3.10** read and comprehend informational texts

TODAY'S

Monday, September 5, 2014

Whose Land Is It?

by Ellen Gold

People and Wild Animals

People and animals need places to live. Animals have lived in the wilderness for thousands of years. They live in ancient forests, oceans, and other habitats. Yet wild animals also live in people's yards. They live in cities, too.

Coyotes are no strangers to cities. One even walked into a restaurant in Chicago. Within moments, a panicking worker had climbed onto the counter.

Running into an unexpected alligator can be horrifying. People may have to take emergency steps, like having a trapper catch the animal.

Habitat Loss

Why are wild animals moving closer to people? They are losing their habitats. Then they must find new places to live.

Fires destroy many animals' homes. Some years are especially fiery. In 2006, fires burned nearly 10 million acres of wild land in the United States.

People destroy habitats, too. People build homes, stores, and roads where wild animals live. In Florida, many homes are near swamps and waterways. These are places where alligators live.

Changing Ways

Alligators have been around since prehistoric times. They mostly fear people. Yet that may be changing. Why is this?

The reason is far from mysterious. Some people feed alligators. Then those alligators stop fearing people. They may think that all people will feed them.

Other animals link people to food, too. Scientific experts know a lot about black bears. Country bears look for food during the day. City bears eat at night. They know that people put out garbage. So, city bears find food in dumpsters and trashcans.

How can people keep bears away? People need to change their habits. They should use bear-proof trashcans. They should fasten the cans immediately after use. If bears can't get food, they won't come back.

This black bear has wandered into someone's backyard garden, right in the heart of a big city. Have wild animals ever visited your home?

Compare Texts

TEXT TO TEXT

Compare Bears With a partner, compare the bears in *Two Bear Cubs* with the bears described in *Whose Land Is It?* In which text are the bears realistic? In which do they act like people? What can you learn about bear behavior from each text? Work together to write your answers. Support your answers with text evidence.

TEXT TO SELF

Connect to Writing *Whose Land Is It*? describes some experiences people have with wild animals. Think about a time you had a funny, scary, or interesting experience with an animal. Write a paragraph that tells what happened.

TEXT TO WORLD

Compare Brothers Think about Older Brother and Younger Brother in *Two Bear Cubs*. Discuss with a partner how they are alike and different. Compare how they act toward each other with how human brothers sometimes act.

Go Digital

COMMON CORE   **RL.3.1** ask and answer questions to demonstrate understanding, referring to the text; **RL.3.3** describe characters and explain how their actions contribute to the sequence of events; **W.3.3b** use dialogue and descriptions to develop experiences and events or show characters' responses; **W.3.10** write routinely over extended time frames or short time frames

Grammar

More Irregular Verbs Some verbs have a special spelling to show past time. They have another spelling when used with *has, have,* or *had.*

Present	Past	With Helping Verbs
go	went	has, have, had gone
see	saw	has, have, had seen
do	did	has, have, had done
run	ran	has, have, had run
come	came	has, have, had come
eat	ate	has, have, had eaten

Try This! **Work with a partner. Read the sentences aloud. Choose the correct verb for each sentence.**

❶ The bears (go, went) to the river and caught fish.

❷ The brothers (run, ran) and played.

❸ Older Brother has (ate, eaten) too many berries.

❹ Younger Brother (saw, seen) a big, flat rock.

❺ Their mother (did, done) not know how to find her cubs.

When you write, it is important to use exact verbs. Your readers will understand your writing better. Exact verbs will also make your writing more interesting.

Less Exact Verb	Exact Verb
The mice ran away from the giant dog.	The mice dashed away from the giant dog. The mice darted away from the giant dog. The mice scampered away from the giant dog.

Connect Grammar to Writing

As you revise your persuasive essay next week, look for places where you can use exact verbs.

COMMON CORE **W.3.1a** introduce the topic, state an opinion, and create an organizational structure; **W.3.1b** provide reasons that support the opinion; **W.3.1d** provide a concluding statement or section; **W.3.4** produce writing in which development and organization are appropriate to task and purpose; **W.3.5** develop and strengthen writing by planning, revising, and editing

Opinion Writing

Reading-Writing Workshop: Prewrite

✔ **Ideas** When you write a **persuasive essay,** picture your readers asking, "Why should I do what you want?" To explore ideas, think of at least three reasons why readers should accept your opinion. Then list your reasons in an order that makes sense.

Daniel wanted to persuade other kids to join a club. He listed reasons. Then he organized his ideas in a list by starting with the strongest reason and adding details.

Writing Process Checklist

▶ **Prewrite**

☑ **Did I think about my audience, or readers?**

☑ **Did I decide on my opinion about the topic?**

☑ **Did I give reasons that will persuade my audience?**

☑ **Did I order my reasons?**

Draft

Revise

Edit

Publish and Share

Exploring the Topic

Why You Should Join the Penguin Club

• It's fun and interesting.

• You meet new people.

• ~~Some kids have quit.~~

• Penguins need help.

162

Prewriting Outline

My Opinion: Children should join the Penguin Club.

Reason: It's fun and interesting!

Details: learn cool facts

go to Science Museum

see live penguins at Aquarium

Reason: Penguins need help.

Details: fewer places to live

dogs hunt penguins

oil spills

Reason: You'll meet new people.

Details: kids are nice and love animals

meet our leader, Mr. Spears

Reading as a Writer

Which details would persuade you to join Daniel's club? What details can you add to your own outline to persuade your readers?

I picked my best reasons and chose an order for them. Then I added details.

✅ TARGET VOCABULARY

shelter
colony
constant
wilderness
climate
region
unexpected
gliding
overheated
layer

Vocabulary Reader

Context Cards

COMMON CORE

L.3.6 acquire and use conversational, general academic, and domain-specific words and phrases

Vocabulary in Context

1 shelter

A tent can make a good shelter for an explorer. It is a good place to keep warm.

2 colony

Some people take trips to study a colony, or large group, of penguins.

3 constant

Steady, or constant, rain can make hiking trails slippery and difficult to use.

4 wilderness

Explorers often travel through wilderness, or unsettled areas.

Go Digital

▶ Study each Context Card.

▶ Place the Vocabulary words in alphabetical order.

5 climate

Boaters must avoid ice when exploring regions with a very cold climate.

6 region

This overgrown jungle is in a hot and rainy region, or area.

7 unexpected

The unexpected view from the top surprised these hikers.

8 gliding

Gliding, or moving smoothly, through the air is an exciting way to explore.

9 overheated

Smart explorers find shade and drink water when they feel overheated.

10 layer

A layer of ice must be several inches thick before it is safe to cross.

Read and Comprehend

Go Digital

Main Ideas and Details As you read *Life on the Ice*, look for the **main ideas,** or the most important points the author makes. Look for **supporting details,** including facts and examples, that provide more information. Note how this text evidence supports the main ideas. Use a graphic organizer like this one to help you.

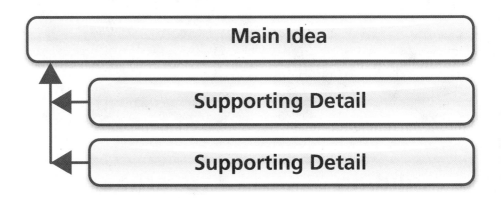

Main Idea

Supporting Detail

Supporting Detail

☑ **TARGET STRATEGY**

Infer/Predict As you read *Life on the Ice*, think about what the author is telling you and **predict** what information you will learn. Make your predictions based on text evidence.

Climate

Climate is the long-term weather in a certain area of Earth. The climate of Florida, for example, is hot in the summer and mild most of the winter. It also rains in all seasons of the year.

The climate of a place affects how people live. In Florida, people can go outside most days. They can wear lightweight clothes for much of the year. What happens when the weather is often 30 degrees Fahrenheit or more below zero and a warm day is just above freezing? How do people adjust to that kind of climate? How do they even survive it?

Bundle up and read *Life on the Ice* to learn answers to these questions.

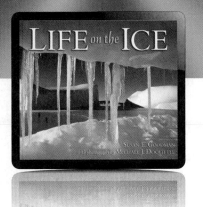

LIFE on the ICE

SUSAN E. GOODMAN
with photographs by MICHAEL J. DOOLITTLE

✓ TARGET SKILL

Main Ideas and Details
Tell important ideas and details about a topic.

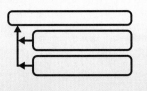

✓ GENRE

Informational text gives you facts and information about a topic. As you read, look for:

▶ photographs and captions
▶ important details that support big ideas about a topic

COMMON CORE
RI.3.2 determine the main idea/recount details and explain how they support the main idea; **RI.3.10** read and comprehend informational texts; **L.3.5a** distinguish the literal and nonliteral meanings of words and phrases in context

MEET THE AUTHOR

SUSAN E. GOODMAN

Susan Goodman's life as a writer has taken her on some exciting adventures. She has gone swimming with dolphins in Florida, made friends with animals in the Amazon rain forest, ridden roller coasters in Pennsylvania, and stayed overnight in an underwater hotel.

MEET THE PHOTOGRAPHER

MICHAEL J. DOOLITTLE

To capture the photos for *Life on the Ice*, Michael Doolittle traveled to the Arctic Circle. He had to keep his camera inside his heavy coat to prevent it from freezing. Doolittle has collaborated with Susan Goodman on many books, including the whole *Ultimate Field Trip* series.

Go Digital

LIFE on the ICE

by SUSAN E. GOODMAN
with photographs by MICHAEL J. DOOLITTLE

The top and the bottom of our planet are covered with ice. The top, the Arctic, is home to the North Pole. It can be so cold that a cup of hot water, thrown in the air, will explode into a cloud of ice particles.

The North Pole is located in the middle of the Arctic Ocean and is usually covered by ice.

The South Pole is at the bottom of our planet on the continent of Antarctica. This region is even colder than the Arctic, sometimes plunging to −125°F (−87.2°C). In winter, parts of the oceans surrounding Antarctica freeze over, doubling its size. Antarctica is the coldest, driest, windiest place on Earth. It is so isolated that no human had even seen this continent until two hundred years ago.

The ice covering Antarctica contains about 70 percent of the world's freshwater.

ANALYZE THE TEXT

Main Ideas and Details Which details on this page help support the main idea that Antarctica is an extremely cold place?

Places this cold, this extreme, are hard to imagine. In fall the sun sets and doesn't rise again for the entire winter. Months later, it shines twenty-four hours a day—all summer long.

Even though they are covered by ice, these regions are deserts—dry like the Sahara. Very little snow falls in either place. But when it does, it rarely melts. Over time, the snow becomes ice—in some places, almost three miles (5 km) thick.

Icebergs can be as small as a piano or larger than a small country.

This ice is slowly moving, inching from the middle of the Arctic and Antarctica to their coasts. By the time pieces break off into the ocean and become icebergs, the ice is 100,000 years old.

People fly thousands of miles to reach the Poles. And when the winds kick up and blow the snow around, it's hard to know where the sky ends and the land begins. Pilots say that it's like flying inside a Ping-Pong ball.

Many of the instruments normally used to guide planes won't work there. In fact, navigators flying to the Poles are the only ones left in the U.S. Air Force who still help map their route with the stars. This is some of the hardest flying there is.

ANALYZE THE TEXT

Literal and Nonliteral Meanings What do the pilots mean when they say that flying in the Poles is like flying inside a Ping-Pong ball?

Planes do not land in these wintry worlds by rolling down concrete runways. They use skis instead. And they slide like giant sleds until they stop. Gliding along, the skis get so hot that they melt the snow they're resting on. Pilots must pull them up when the planes stop. Otherwise, the wet snow would refreeze on the skis and the planes would be stuck to the ground.

When pilots land at the South Pole, they keep their engines running. It's so cold that they might not start up again.

It sounds like an adventure story, doesn't it? It *is* an adventure story—one with science. Scientists are today's explorers, braving the wilderness to learn more about our world.

The snow near the North Pole, for example, hasn't melted since the last ice age. Over 100,000 years of it has been pressed into an ice sheet almost 2 miles (3.2 km) thick. But each layer looks separate, like the rings of a tree.

Some scientists use this snow to measure air pollution. Others are drilling through this ice to pull out history. Each sample they bring up tells a story about the time when it was formed. Scientists have found volcanic ash from Italy's Mount Vesuvius, for instance, and pollution from ancient Roman times.

Scientists began this experiment to learn more about how ice ages begin and end. Before, they thought our climate needed thousands of years to change. Now they know it can happen much, much faster.

Summit Snow 01
1671

At the South Pole some scientists search for meteorites, rocks from outer space. Meteorites are no more likely to fall there than anywhere else on Earth. But, as one scientist explains, if you want to find something dark, it's easier to look on a big white sheet. His team has given thousands of meteorites to our space agency, the National Aeronautics and Space Administration (NASA), for study.

The Antarctic sky is a perfect window to the stars, the best on this planet. It is very clear because it's so cold and dry—and has a night that is six months long. Some scientists use telescopes to study the age of the universe. Others fly balloons to measure rays coming in from outer space.

At the Poles people wear many layers of clothing to keep warmth in and wind out. They wear big boots and overalls called fat-boy pants. Their mittens have furry backs to wipe their noses and warm their ears.

They also wear goggles. Without them, their eyes would get sunburned and temporarily blinded by the strong light bouncing off the snow.

No wearing rings, earrings, or sunglasses with metal frames in the extreme cold. Metal gets so cold that it will freeze any skin that it touches.

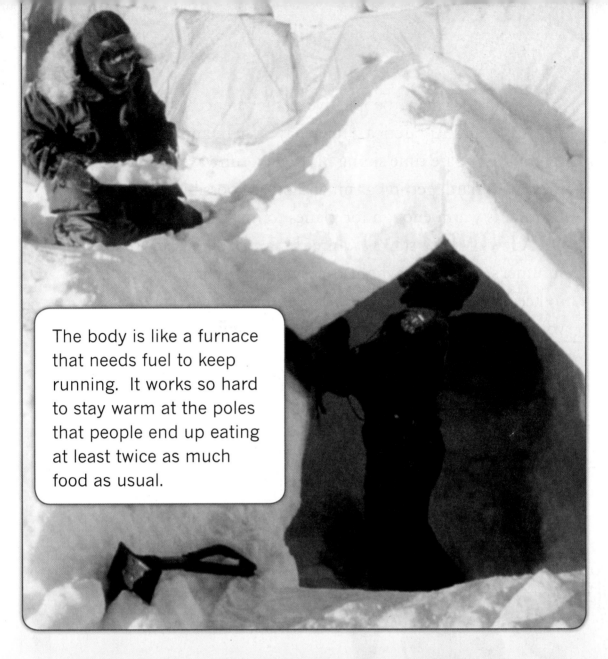

The body is like a furnace that needs fuel to keep running. It works so hard to stay warm at the poles that people end up eating at least twice as much food as usual.

People who work at the Poles must learn how to survive being stuck outdoors. On an unexpected "camping trip," they first build a quick shelter to get out of the wind. Then they build a better one and pack in close to one another, using body heat to stay warm.

Building shelters—doing any work—is much harder in extreme cold. Mittens are very bulky, but it's unsafe to go bare-handed for long. Getting too cold is dangerous, but so is getting overheated. Sweat can freeze into a layer of ice next to your body.

In summer many people live at the science stations in the Arctic and Antarctica. They have a gym and videos and spend their spare time skiing on the icy runways. But mostly they work hard, getting as much done as possible while the weather is warm enough for planes to fly in and out.

A few of them stay all winter long. Scientists say that summer's constant daylight tricks your body into wanting to keep going without rest. But in winter's endless darkness, you feel tired much of the time. One scientist even studies the people who winter-over at the South Pole. He wants to know what kind of person works well in such a small, isolated group. Someday his findings may help pick the people to live in a colony on Mars.

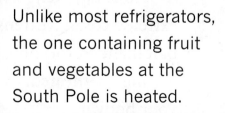

Unlike most refrigerators, the one containing fruit and vegetables at the South Pole is heated.

In spring in Antarctica, the temperature finally climbs up to +10°F (–10°C) and it's warm enough for planes to fly in again. The scientists are eager to get on board and return to the colors and smells of the "green world." Once they buckle up, there is one last frosty problem to solve. The airplane must go 100 miles (160 km) per hour to take off, no easy task when sliding over ice. Sometimes pilots must travel 2 miles (3 km) to reach that speed. And sometimes they need extra help. Then they turn to the eight rockets attached to their plane.

A flick of the switch, a burst of flames and speed, and they are on their way home.

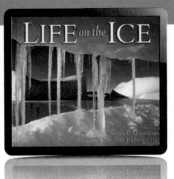

Dig Deeper

How to Analyze the Text

Use these pages to learn about Main Ideas and Details and Literal and Nonliteral Meanings. Then read *Life on the Ice* again to apply what you learned.

Main Ideas and Details

Life on the Ice gives information about what scientists do and the challenges they face in Antarctica. The most important idea about the topic is called the **main idea.** Each paragraph or group of paragraphs is also organized around a main idea. **Supporting details** are facts and examples the author uses to tell more about each main idea.

Look back at pages 174–175 in *Life on the Ice*. In the first paragraph on page 174, you will read the main idea for this section. As you read, you will find supporting details that explain why flying to the Poles is so difficult.

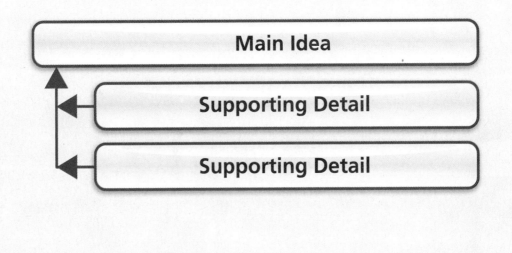

Main Idea

Supporting Detail

Supporting Detail

COMMON CORE **RI.3.2** determine the main idea/recount details and explain how they support the main idea; **L.3.5a** distinguish the literal and nonliteral meanings of words and phrases in context

Literal and Nonliteral Meanings

Words and phrases have exact meanings, also called **literal meanings.** For example, the literal meaning of *sheet* is "a large cloth used to cover a bed."

Words and phrases can also have **nonliteral meanings.** Scientists look for meteorites at the South Pole because, "if you want to find something dark, it's easier to look on a big white sheet." Here the phrase *a big white sheet* has a nonliteral meaning. The author means that the snow covers the ground the same way that a sheet covers a bed. The **context,** or sentences around the phrase, shows that *sheet* is being used in a nonliteral or figurative way.

Your Turn

Turn and Talk Review the selection with a partner to prepare to discuss this question: *What are the coldest places on Earth like?* As you discuss the question, look for text evidence in the selection to support your ideas.

Classroom Conversation

Continue your discussion of *Life on the Ice* by explaining your answers to these questions:

1. Which climate is more challenging for humans, the North Pole's or the South Pole's?

2. Do you think you could work at either of the Poles? Use text evidence to explain why or why not.

3. Why would working in Antarctica be good preparation for an astronaut who plans to go to Mars?

WRITE ABOUT READING

Response The selection discusses many jobs that scientists do. Which job looks most interesting to you? Write a paragraph about the job you would choose and explain your choice. Use main ideas and text evidence to support your opinion and reasons.

Writing Tip

State your opinion at the beginning of your paragraph. Use transition words such as *because* and *so* to link your reasons to your opinion.

COMMON CORE **RI.3.1** ask and answer questions to demonstrate understanding, referring to the text; **RI.3.2** determine the main idea/recount details and explain how they support the main idea; **W.3.1a** introduce the topic, state an opinion, and create an organizational structure; **W.3.1b** provide reasons that support the opinion; **W.3.1c** use linking words and phrases to connect opinion and reasons; **W.3.1d** provide a concluding statement or section; **SL.3.1a** come to discussions prepared/explicitly draw on preparation and other information about the topic; **SL.3.1d** explain own ideas and understanding in light of the discussion

MYTH

☑ GENRE

A **myth,** such as this Readers' Theater, is a story that tells what a group of people believes about the world.

☑ TEXT FOCUS

The **story message** of a myth may explain why or how something in nature came to be.

COMMON CORE **RL.3.2** recount stories and determine the message, lesson, or moral; **RL.3.10** read and comprehend literature

Readers' Theater

The Raven:
An Inuit Myth

retold by Peter Case

Cast of Characters

Narrator	Person
Old Man	Raven

Narrator: Long ago, the People lived in darkness. There was no sun to help things grow. The People called to Raven for help.

Person: Oh, Raven, help us. Our lives are a constant struggle.

Raven: I have heard of an Old Man who has two glowing globes of light. I will try to get these globes.

Narrator: Raven went gliding over the dark wilderness. He came to the shelter where the Old Man lived with his daughter. There, Raven turned himself into a human child.

Old Man: I have a grandson! How wonderful!

Narrator: Raven spoke in the voice of a small child.

Raven: May I please play with the globes of light?

Old Man: Here, grandson, you can play with them.

Narrator: Raven thought of a trick to steal the globes. He pretended he was overheated inside the warm shelter.

Raven: It's so hot inside. I want to take the globes outside.

Old Man: Yes, grandson. You can play outside with the globes.

Narrator: Once Raven was outside, he put on his layer of feathers and flew off with the globes.

Narrator: When he got back to the colony of People, Raven threw the globes up into the sky. One became the sun and the other became the moon. The People were overjoyed.

Person: Now the climate will be good for growing food in this region of the world. Thank you, Raven, for the gift of the sun and for the unexpected gift of the moon.

Compare Texts

Discuss the Sun Think about why the sun is important to the scientists in *Life on the Ice* and to the people in *The Raven*. In a small group, use text evidence to discuss and explain your ideas. Listen carefully to each other. Ask questions if you are not sure about something.

Write a Story Imagine that you are a scientist in Antarctica. Write a short story that tells about your adventures there. Include details about characters and setting and an ending that solves a problem in the story.

Compare Photographs Study the photos in *Life on the Ice*. Think about what you know about your own state's land and climate. Compare and contrast the land and climate at the Poles with those in your state. Use details in the pictures and text to support your ideas.

COMMON CORE **RI.3.7** use information gained from illustrations and words to demonstrate understanding; **SL.3.1a** come to discussions prepared/explicitly draw on preparation and other information about the topic; **SL.3.1c** ask questions to check understanding, stay on topic, and link comments to others' remarks; **SL.3.1d** explain own ideas and understanding in light of the discussion

Grammar

What Is an Adverb? An adverb is a word that describes a verb. Adverbs can tell *how, when,* or *where* an action happens. Adverbs can come before or after the verbs they describe.

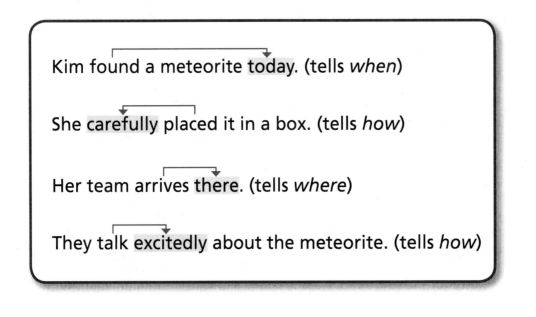

Kim found a meteorite today. (tells *when*)

She carefully placed it in a box. (tells *how*)

Her team arrives there. (tells *where*)

They talk excitedly about the meteorite. (tells *how*)

Try This! Work with a partner. Read the sentences aloud. Find the adverb in each sentence.

1. Alex ran ahead.

2. He reached the campsite first.

3. He eagerly searched for Dr. Keller.

4. He looked everywhere for his friend.

5. Alex found Dr. Keller skiing happily on the trail.

Short, choppy sentences can be combined to make your writing smoother. Combine two sentences by moving an adverb. Often you can choose where to place the adverb in the new sentence.

Two Sentences

I received a new scarf.

I received it yesterday.

Combined Sentence

I received a new scarf yesterday.

Yesterday, I received a new scarf.

Two sentences: I wrap my scarf around my neck.
I wrap my scarf snugly.

Combined sentence: I wrap my scarf snugly around my neck.

Connect Grammar to Writing

As you revise your persuasive essay, think about combining sentences by moving an adverb.

W.3.1a introduce the topic, state an opinion, and create an organizational structure; **W.3.1b** provide reasons that support the opinion; **W.3.1c** use linking words and phrases to connect opinion and reasons; **W.3.1d** provide a concluding statement or section; **W.3.5** develop and strengthen writing by planning, revising, and editing

COMMON CORE

Opinion Writing

Reading–Writing Workshop: Revise

✓ **Ideas**   A **persuasive essay** explains in detail the reasons for the writer's opinion. To help readers follow along, each reason has its own paragraph, starting with a transition word, such as *another*.

Daniel drafted his essay about joining a club. Later, he separated his reasons into paragraphs and added transition words.

my WriteSmart

Go Digital

Writing Process Checklist

Prewrite

Draft

▶ **Revise**

✓ Did I begin by telling my opinion?

✓ Did I give strong reasons?

✓ Did I support my reasons with details and examples?

✓ Do my new paragraphs use transition words?

✓ Did I sum up my reasons in a concluding statement?

Edit

Publish and Share

Revised Draft

Do you love penguins? If your answer
is yes, join the Penguin Club! ¶The main reason to join is that It's fun and

interesting. We visit the penguin exhibit

at the Science Museum, see live penguins

at the Aquarium, and do projects. You'll

learn lots of cool penguin facts. For

example, did you know that penguins go
¶Another great reason to join the club is that
sledding on their stomachs? Penguins

need your help.

The Penguin Club Is Cool!

by Daniel Boyd

Do you love penguins? If your answer is yes, join the Penguin Club!

The main reason to join is that it's fun and interesting. We visit the penguin exhibit at the Science Museum, see live penguins at the Aquarium, and do projects. You'll learn lots of cool penguin facts. For example, did you know that penguins go sledding on their stomachs?

Another great reason to join the club is that penguins need your help. In some parts of the world, penguins have fewer safe, healthy places to live because of changes caused by people.

These are the main reasons why I joined the Penguin Club. I think that most kids would enjoy the club. You can make new friends while doing things to help the penguins.

Reading as a Writer

Why did Daniel divide his essay into paragraphs? In your essay, where should you divide your writing into paragraphs?

I began a new paragraph for each reason. I was also careful to write contractions correctly.

Test POWER

Read the stories "Coyote and Eagle Steal the Sun and Moon" and "Why the Sun and the Moon Live in the Sky." As you read, stop and answer each question using text evidence.

Coyote and Eagle Steal the Sun and Moon: A Zuni Folktale

The Zuni are an American Indian people of New Mexico and Arizona. Animals and nature are an important part of Zuni stories.

Long ago, the land was always dark, and the weather was always warm. One day, Eagle and Coyote were hungry, so they went out to hunt for food. Hunting was difficult because there was no daylight.

After a while, Eagle and Coyote came to the home of the powerful Kachina people. The Kachinas owned a shining box that held the sun and the moon. If Eagle and Coyote had the shining light of the sun and the moon, they would not have to hunt in the dark. They decided they must have that box.

The two hunters waited until the Kachinas were asleep. Then they seized the shining box and crept silently away. Eagle was the first to carry the box, but after a while Coyote offered to take a turn. Eagle handed his friend the box, and they continued on their way.

> **1** What does the word *seized* mean? Explain how you can figure out the meaning from the way the word is used in the story.

COMMON CORE

RL.3.1 ask and answer questions to demonstrate understanding, referring to the text; **RL.3.2** recount stories and determine the message, lesson, or moral; **RL.3.4** determine the meaning of words and phrases, distinguishing literal from nonliteral language; **RL.3.6** distinguish own point of view from the narrator or characters' point of view

Coyote was a curious creature, however. He was so eager to see what was in the box that he couldn't resist tipping open the lid just a little bit.

Out flew the sun! Out flew the moon! Up into the sky they went, as Eagle and Coyote watched in amazement.

Ever since that time, the sun and the moon have remained in the sky, giving light and warmth to the land below. Because they flew so far into the sky, Earth has less heat than it did before. That is why we now have winter during part of the year.

> **2** What does this folktale explain about nature?
> Use details from the story to support your response.

Why the Sun and Moon Live in the Sky: A Nigerian Folktale

This story comes from Nigeria, a country in western Africa. Like many folktales, it tells how something in nature came to be.

A long, long time ago, Sun and Moon lived on Earth. They often visited their good friend Water, but Water never came to visit them. Water said it was because their house was too small. "You will need a very large house," Water told them, "as my people are numerous and take up much room."

So Sun and Moon built an enormous house and invited Water to visit. When Water arrived, one of his people called out, "Are you sure it is safe for Water to enter?" Sun and Moon replied that their friend was most welcome and they were sure it would be safe.

Then the water began flowing in, with all the fish and turtles and other sorts of water creatures. Soon the water in the house was up to a person's knees. Water asked, "Are you sure you want us all to come in?" Sun and Moon politely said yes.

More and more water flowed into the house, bringing more and more water creatures. Now the water was as high as a person's head. Water asked if they were sure it was safe for even more of his people to come in. Sun and Moon politely said yes.

> **3** Do you agree or disagree with Sun and Moon that it is safe for more of Water's people to come in? Use details from the story to explain your response.

Before long, the water was so deep that Sun and Moon had to sit on the roof of their house. Water asked again if it was all right for more to come in. Sun and Moon politely said yes.

Before long, the water had reached the roof and was still continuing to rise. Sun and Moon had no place to go now except into the sky. So up they went, and there they have remained ever since.

> **4** How are the two stories you have read alike, and how are they different?

unit 5

Vocabulary in Context

☑ TARGET VOCABULARY

prairie
slick
fetch
clattered
sniff
rough
thumped
batted
buzzing
rustle

COMMON CORE L.3.6 acquire and use conversational, general academic, and domain-specific words and phrases

1 prairie

Few trees can be found on the flat or rolling land of the prairie.

2 slick

Walk carefully! The ice is slick and you may fall easily.

3 fetch

She took buckets to fetch water for the animals to drink.

4 clattered

The children covered their ears when the horse and carriage clattered by.

Go Digital

▶ Study each Context Card.

▶ Make up a new context sentence that uses two Vocabulary words.

5 sniff

The skunk stopped to sniff, or smell, the flower. It had a nice scent.

6 rough

Ouch! The bark on the old tree is rough to the touch.

7 thumped

The children thumped their feet as they learned the steps of the dance.

8 batted

The curious puppy batted, or hit, the sock with its paw.

9 buzzing

After buzzing around, this bee landed on a wildflower.

10 rustle

Walking through piles of dry leaves makes a soft rustle.

Read and Comprehend

☑ TARGET SKILL

Story Structure As you read *Sarah, Plain and Tall*, note details about the characters, setting, and plot. Record text evidence to help you describe how the **actions** of a character can affect **events** within the story.

Setting	Characters
Plot	

☑ TARGET STRATEGY

Monitor/Clarify As you read, **monitor,** or think about, whether you understand what you are reading. If there is something you do not understand, find a way to **clarify** it, or to make it clear.

Pioneer Life

The pioneers were brave, independent people who left their homes in cities, villages, and farms in the East to move to the West. The western lands were mostly unknown. There were no roads to guide new settlers and no towns to welcome them.

The pioneers risked great danger to move to the West. Once they found a place to settle, they had to be self-sufficient. They lived far from towns and from other settlers. Their courage is a quality that Americans still celebrate today. In *Sarah, Plain and Tall*, you'll read about the changes one of these pioneer families faces.

ANCHOR TEXT

Sarah,
Plain and Tall

✓ TARGET SKILL

Story Structure Identify the characters, setting, and plot of the story. Think about how each character's actions affect story events.

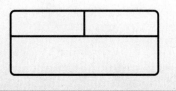

✓ GENRE

Historical fiction is a story that is set in the past. As you read, look for:

▶ a setting that is a real time and place in the past
▶ realistic characters and events
▶ details that show the story took place in the past

RL.3.3 describe characters and explain how their actions contribute to the sequence of events; **RL.3.10** read and comprehend literature

MEET THE AUTHOR

Patricia MacLachlan

As a child, Patricia MacLachlan loved to read. She never imagined that she would be a writer one day. *Sarah, Plain and Tall* is based on the life of a real person. MacLachlan's mother knew the real Sarah, who was married to one of her family members. In fact, as the book grew and changed, MacLachlan added details from her own life. Parts of the story also come from the lives of MacLachlan's parents, husband, and children.

MacLachlan says that children often ask her why she writes. She writes for the same reasons that people read—to find out what happens and to find out more about herself.

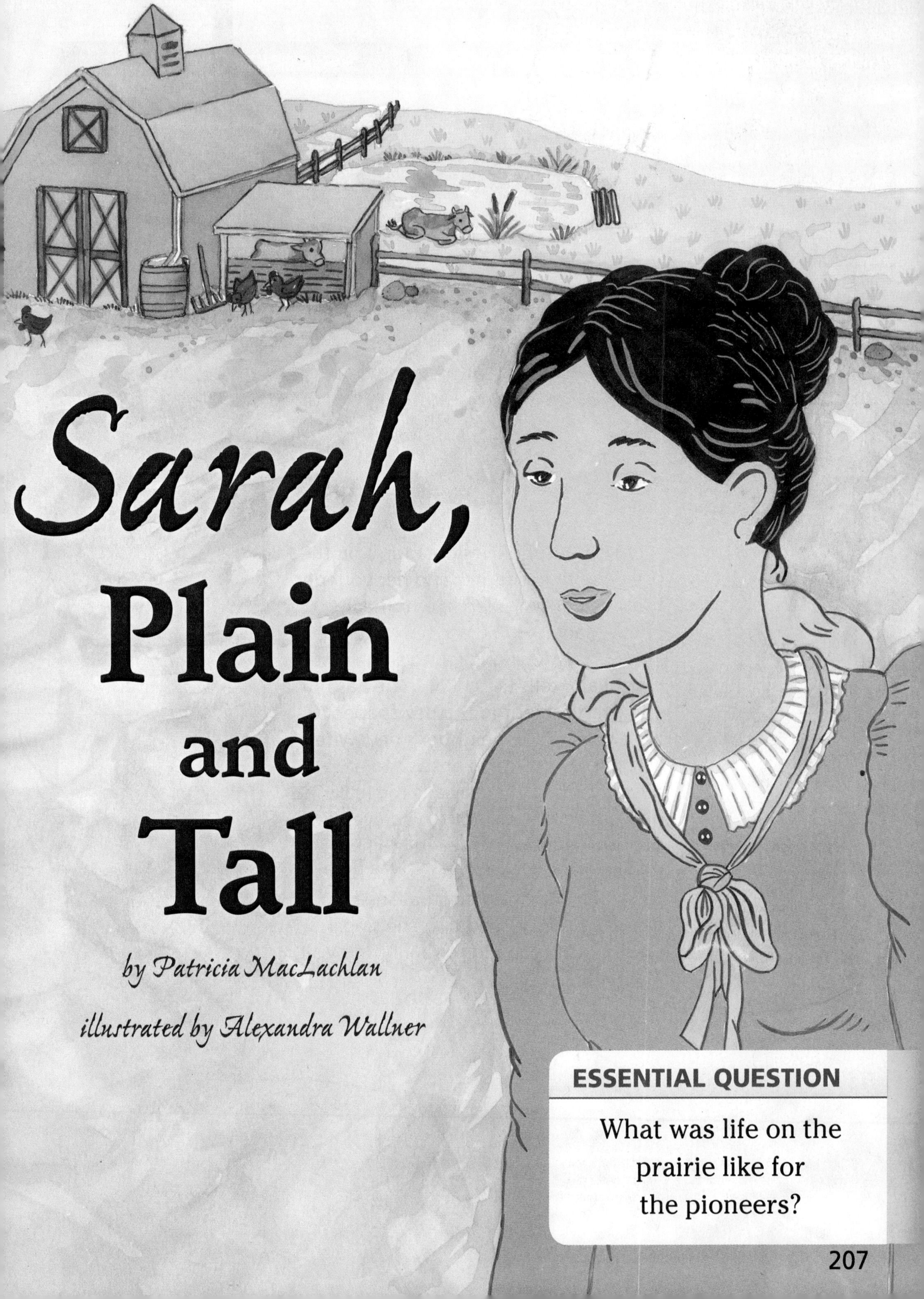

Sarah, Plain and Tall

by Patricia MacLachlan

illustrated by Alexandra Wallner

ESSENTIAL QUESTION

What was life on the prairie like for the pioneers?

Anna Witting lives on a farm on the prairie with her father and her younger brother, Caleb. Caleb likes to hear about Mama, who died soon after he was born and who loved to sing. One night Papa tells the children he has put an advertisement in the newspaper for a wife. Their neighbor's new wife, Maggie, had come in answer to an advertisement. Papa reads the letter he has received from Sarah, who lives with her brother near the sea in Maine.

Papa, Anna, and Caleb write letters to Sarah. They find out that she has a cat named Seal and that she sings. Now Sarah is coming for a month's visit, "to see how it is."

Sarah came in the spring. She came through green grass fields that bloomed with Indian paintbrush, red and orange, and blue-eyed grass.

Papa got up early for the long day's trip to the train and back. He brushed his hair so slick and shiny that Caleb laughed. He wore a clean blue shirt, and a belt instead of suspenders.

He fed and watered the horses, talking to them as he hitched them up to the wagon. Old Bess, calm and kind; Jack, wild-eyed, reaching over to nip Bess on the neck.

"Clear day, Bess," said Papa, rubbing her nose.

"Settle down, Jack." He leaned his head on Jack.

And then Papa drove off along the dirt road to fetch Sarah. Papa's new wife. Maybe. Maybe our new mother.

Gophers ran back and forth across the road, stopping to stand up and watch the wagon. Far off in the field a woodchuck ate and listened. Ate and listened.

Caleb and I did our chores without talking. We shoveled out the stalls and laid down new hay. We fed the sheep. We swept and straightened and carried wood and water. And then our chores were done.

Caleb pulled on my shirt.

"Is my face clean?" he asked. "Can my face be *too* clean?" He looked alarmed.

"No, your face is clean but not too clean," I said.

Caleb slipped his hand into mine as we stood on the porch, watching the road. He was afraid.

"Will she be nice?" he asked. "Like Maggie?"

"Sarah will be nice," I told him.

"How far away is Maine?" he asked.

"You know how far. Far away, by the sea."

"Will Sarah bring some sea?" he asked.

"No, you cannot bring the sea."

The sheep ran in the field, and far off the cows moved slowly to the pond, like turtles.

"Will she like us?" asked Caleb very softly.

I watched a marsh hawk wheel down behind the barn.

He looked up at me.

"Of course she will like us." He answered his own question. "We are nice," he added, making me smile.

We waited and watched. I rocked on the porch and Caleb rolled a marble on the wood floor. Back and forth. Back and forth. The marble was blue.

We saw the dust from the wagon first, rising above the road, above the heads of Jack and Old Bess. Caleb climbed up onto the porch roof and shaded his eyes.

"A bonnet!" he cried. "I see a yellow bonnet!"

The dogs came out from under the porch, ears up, their eyes on the cloud of dust bringing Sarah. The wagon passed the fenced field, and the cows and sheep looked up, too. It rounded the windmill and the barn and the windbreak of Russian olive that Mama had planted long ago. Nick began to bark, then Lottie, and the wagon clattered into the yard and stopped by the steps.

"Hush," said Papa to the dogs.

And it was quiet.

Sarah stepped down from the wagon, a cloth bag in her hand. She reached up and took off her yellow bonnet, smoothing back her brown hair into a bun. She was plain and tall.

"Did you bring some sea?" cried Caleb beside me.

"Something from the sea," said Sarah, smiling. "And me." She turned and lifted a black case from the wagon. "And Seal, too."

Carefully she opened the case, and Seal, gray with white feet, stepped out. Lottie lay down, her head on her paws, staring. Nick leaned down to sniff. Then he lay down, too.

"The cat will be good in the barn," said Papa. "For mice."

Sarah smiled. "She will be good in the house, too."

Sarah took Caleb's hand, then mine. Her hands were large and rough. She gave Caleb a shell—a moon snail, she called it—that was curled and smelled of salt.

"The gulls fly high and drop the shells on the rocks below," she told Caleb. "When the shell is broken, they eat what is inside."

"That is very smart," said Caleb.

"For you, Anna," said Sarah, "a sea stone."

And she gave me the smoothest and whitest stone I had ever seen.

"The sea washes over and over and around the stone, rolling it until it is round and perfect."

"That is very smart, too," said Caleb. He looked up at Sarah. "We do not have the sea here."

Sarah turned and looked out over the plains.

"No," she said. "There is no sea here. But the land rolls a little like the sea."

My father did not see her look, but I did. And I knew that Caleb had seen it, too. Sarah was not smiling. Sarah was already lonely. In a month's time the preacher might come to marry Sarah and Papa. And a month was a long time. Time enough for her to change her mind and leave us.

Papa took Sarah's bags inside, where her room was ready with a quilt on the bed and blue flax dried in a vase on the night table.

Seal stretched and made a small cat sound. I watched her circle the dogs and sniff the air. Caleb came out and stood beside me.

"When will we sing?" he whispered.

I shook my head, turning the white stone over and over in my hand. I wished everything was as perfect as the stone. I wished that Papa and Caleb and I were perfect for Sarah. I wished we had a sea of our own.

ANALYZE THE TEXT

Story Structure What actions led to Sarah's arrival on the prairie?

The dogs loved Sarah first. Lottie slept beside her bed, curled in a soft circle, and Nick leaned his face on the covers in the morning, watching for the first sign that Sarah was awake. No one knew where Seal slept. Seal was a roamer.

Sarah's collection of shells sat on the windowsill.

"A scallop," she told us, picking up the shells one by one, "a sea clam, an oyster, a razor clam. And a conch shell. If you put it to your ear you can hear the sea." She put it to Caleb's ear, then mine. Papa listened, too. Then Sarah listened once more, with a look so sad and far away that Caleb leaned against me.

"At least Sarah can hear the sea," he whispered.

Papa was quiet and shy with Sarah, and so was I. But Caleb talked to Sarah from morning until the light left the sky.

"Where are you going?" he asked. "To do what?"

"To pick flowers," said Sarah. "I'll hang some of them upside down and dry them so they'll keep some color. And we can have flowers all winter long."

"I'll come, too!" cried Caleb. "Sarah said winter," he said to me. "That means Sarah will stay."

Together we picked flowers, paintbrush and clover and prairie violets. There were buds on the wild roses that climbed up the paddock fence.

"The roses will bloom in early summer," I told Sarah. I looked to see if she knew what I was thinking. Summer was when the wedding would be. *Might* be. Sarah and Papa's wedding.

ANALYZE THE TEXT

Point of View What does Anna think of Sarah so far? Do you have the same point of view?

We hung the flowers from the ceiling in little bunches. "I've never seen this before," said Sarah. "What is it called?"

"Bride's bonnet," I told her.

Caleb smiled at the name.

"We don't have this by the sea," she said. "We have seaside goldenrod and wild asters and woolly ragwort."

"Woolly ragwort!" Caleb whooped. He made up a song.

"Woolly ragwort all around,
Woolly ragwort on the ground.
Woolly ragwort grows and grows,
Wolly ragwort in your nose."

Sarah and Papa laughed, and the dogs lifted their heads and thumped their tails against the wood floor. Seal sat on a kitchen chair and watched us with yellow eyes.

We ate Sarah's stew, the late light coming through the windows. Papa had baked bread that was still warm from the fire.

"The stew is fine," said Papa.

"Ayuh." Sarah nodded. "The bread, too."

"What does 'ayuh' mean?" asked Caleb.

"In Maine it means yes," said Sarah. "Do you want more stew?"

"Ayuh," said Caleb.

"Ayuh," echoed my father.

After dinner Sarah told us about William. "He has a gray-and-white boat named *Kittiwake*." She looked out the window. "That is a small gull found way off the shore where William fishes. There are three aunts who live near us. They wear silk dresses and no shoes. You would love them."

"Ayuh," said Caleb.

"Does your brother look like you?" I asked.

"Yes," said Sarah. "He is plain and tall."

At dusk Sarah cut Caleb's hair on the front steps, gathering his curls and scattering them on the fence and ground. Seal batted some hair around the porch as the dogs watched.

"Why?" asked Caleb.

"For the birds," said Sarah. "They will use it for their nests. Later we can look for nests of curls."

"Sarah said 'later,'" Caleb whispered to me as we spread his hair about. "Sarah will stay."

Sarah cut Papa's hair, too. No one else saw, but I found him behind the barn, tossing the pieces of hair into the wind for the birds.

Sarah brushed my hair and tied it up in back with a rose velvet ribbon she had brought from Maine. She brushed hers long and free and tied it back, too, and we stood side by side looking into the mirror. I looked taller, like Sarah, and fair and thin. And with my hair pulled back I looked a little like her daughter. Sarah's daughter.

And then it was time for singing.

Sarah sang us a song we had never heard before as we sat on the porch, insects buzzing in the dark, the rustle of cows in the grasses. It was called "Sumer Is Icumen in," and she taught it to us all, even Papa, who sang as if he had never stopped singing.

Sumer is icumen in,
Lhude sing cuccu!

"What is sumer?" asked Caleb. He said it "soomer," the way Sarah had said it.

"Summer," said Papa and Sarah at the same time. Caleb and I looked at each other. Summer was coming.

221

Sarah,
Plain and Tall

Dig Deeper

How to Analyze the Text

Use these pages to learn about Story Structure and Point of View. Then read *Sarah, Plain and Tall* again to apply what you learned.

Story Structure

Historical fiction stories like *Sarah, Plain and Tall* have a **story structure.** The structure is made up of characters, a setting, and a plot. Many of the events in the plot happen as a result of each character's actions. These actions in turn affect what happens next.

Look back at pages 213–214 in *Sarah, Plain and Tall.* When Sarah arrives, she brings gifts from the sea in Maine. How does this action affect the other characters? Read for text evidence to help you describe how this affects events later in the story.

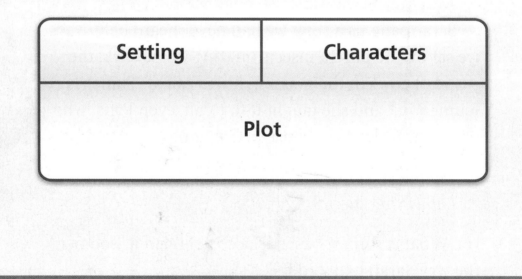

Setting	Characters
Plot	

COMMON CORE **RL.3.1** ask and answer questions to demonstrate understanding, referring to the text; **RL.3.3** describe characters and explain how their actions contribute to the sequence of events; **RL.3.6** distinguish own point of view from the narrator or characters' point of view

Point of View

The **point of view** is the author's message for the reader and can be delivered through the actions, thoughts, words, and feelings of the story's narrator or characters. In fiction stories, authors may use the point of view of the narrator or characters to focus the readers' attention on an important idea, opinion, or feeling from the story.

Readers often have their own point of view about what happens in a story, too. As a reader, you should decide if you agree with the narrator or character or if you have a completely different opinion.

Your Turn

Review the story with a partner to prepare to discuss this question: *What was life on the prairie like for the pioneers?* As you discuss, use text evidence from the story to support your ideas.

Classroom Conversation

Continue your discussion of *Sarah, Plain and Tall* by explaining your answers to these questions:

1. Sarah says the "land rolls a little like the sea." What do you think she means? What do you imagine?

2. For what reasons do you think Sarah would stay after a month's visit? For what reasons might she leave?

3. Explain why Anna wishes her family had a sea of their own.

WRITE ABOUT READING

Response Do you think Sarah stays? Write a paragraph that tells what you think happens. Use text evidence from the story to support your answer. Include a conclusion to sum up your opinion.

Sarah, Plain and Tall

Writing Tip

As you write, pay close attention to verb tenses. You will be writing mostly about what you think happens to Anna and her family in the future.

COMMON CORE **RL.3.3** describe characters and explain how their actions contribute to the sequence of events; **W.3.1a** introduce the topic, state an opinion, and create an organizational structure; **W.3.1b** provide reasons that support the opinion; **W.3.1d** provide a concluding statement or section; **W.3.10** write routinely over extended time frames or short time frames; **SL.3.1a** come to discussions prepared/ explicitly draw on preparation and other information about the topic; **SL.3.1d** explain own ideas and understanding in light of the discussion

225

WAGONS
of the
Old West

✅ **GENRE**

Informational text gives facts and information about a topic.

✅ **TEXT FOCUS**

A **diagram** is an illustration that shows important details, such as how something is made. Labels or captions are often added to tell what the parts of a diagram show.

COMMON CORE **RI.3.7** use information gained from illustrations and words to demonstrate understanding; **RI.3.10** read and comprehend informational texts

WAGONS
of the
Old West

by Maria Santos
illustrated by Dan Bridy

One of the oldest kinds of transportation is the wagon. It is a four-wheeled vehicle drawn by strong animals. People around the world have driven wagons for thousands of years.

Wagons on the Oregon Trail

In the United States, wagons made history between the 1830s and 1860s. During this time, thousands of pioneers traveled westward. Some went as far as Oregon, but others settled in many places along the way.

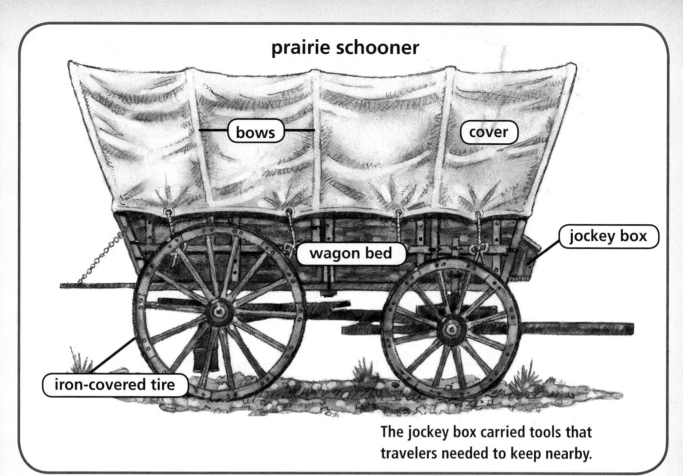

prairie schooner

bows

cover

jockey box

wagon bed

iron-covered tire

The jockey box carried tools that travelers needed to keep nearby.

The pioneers journeyed for up to six months to reach the West Coast. They had to pack a lot of food and supplies for the trip. Families packed some of their furniture, too. To protect their possessions and supplies from the sun and the rain, they used covered wagons.

Back east, there was an enormous wagon known as the Conestoga wagon. Its rear wheels were as tall as a man. The top rose to more than 11 feet above the ground. The back and front of the wagon bed were sloped upward so that cargo would not tip out when traveling across mountains.

People liked the design of the Conestoga, but these wagons were too heavy for the long journey west. They needed as many as six or eight horses to pull them. The wagons would have to travel over very rough land as there were no roads yet.

A smaller wagon was built, with high, sloped ends to keep its cargo from spilling out. It also had a white canvas cover to protect the cargo from sun and rain. Traveling in groups, or "trains," across the flat land of the prairies with their white tops, the wagons sometimes looked like ships. People soon called them "prairie schooners," as a schooner was a type of ship with white sails.

227

Wagons on Prairie Farms

Once the pioneers chose a place to settle, they built houses to sleep in and to store their food. They no longer needed to carry such heavy loads. The prairie schooners were much too big for everyday use. Pioneers needed a wagon that was comfortable to ride on. Much smaller farm wagons were built. Springs were added so that riders would not feel all of the bumps along the trails. A spring is a steel brace that holds up the bed of a wagon. The springs were lighter than the heavy frame of a prairie schooner, so the wagon could travel faster.

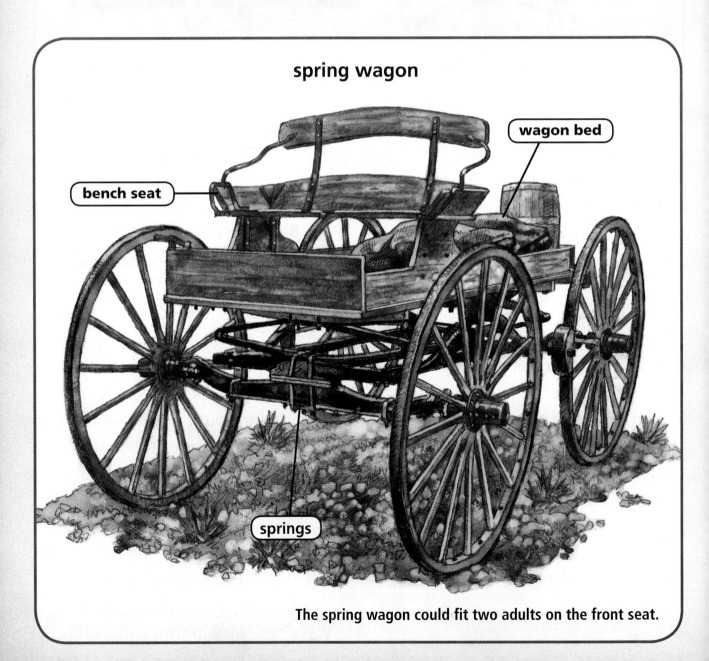

spring wagon

wagon bed

bench seat

springs

The spring wagon could fit two adults on the front seat.

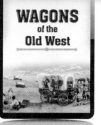

Sarah, Plain and Tall

WAGONS of the **Old West**

Compare Texts

Compare Wagons Talk with a partner about how the wagon in *Sarah, Plain and Tall* is similar to and different from each of the wagons described in *Wagons of the Old West.* Work together to write a comparison of the wagons. Use text evidence from the selections and the art to support your answers.

Write Your Opinion If you could choose between living near the coast like Sarah did or living on the prairie like Anna and Caleb, which would you choose? Write reasons for your opinion.

Research Settlers On the Internet or in reference books, research the people who settled your state. Who were the American Indians who lived in your part of the country? Where did other people come from and why?

Go Digital

COMMON CORE **RL.3.7** explain how illustrations contribute to the words; **RI.3.7** use information gained from illustrations and words to demonstrate understanding; **RI.3.9** compare and contrast important points and details in texts on the same topic; **W.3.7** conduct short research projects that build knowledge about a topic; **W.3.10** write routinely over extended time frames or short time frames

Grammar

Adverbs That Compare Remember that **adverbs** are words that tell when, where, or how something happens. Adverbs are used to describe verbs.

Adverbs can be used to compare actions. To compare two actions, add *-er* to most adverbs. To compare more than two, add *-est*. For adverbs that end in e, drop the e before adding *-er* or *-est*. For those that end in *y*, change the *y* to *i*. For most adverbs that end in *-ly*, use *more* and *most* to compare.

Adverb	Compare Two	Compare More Than Two
slowly	more slowly	most slowly
late	later	latest
early	earlier	earliest
closely	more closely	most closely

 **Copy each sentence. Fill in the blank with the correct form of the adverb in parentheses.**

❶ He walks _____ than I can run. (fast)

❷ She sings _____ of the whole group. (loud)

❸ Jerry arrived _____ than Ben did. (late)

❹ He drove _____ than the first driver. (carefully)

If you use the wrong adverb form to compare, you can confuse your readers. When you proofread your writing, check that you have used the correct adverb forms to compare two actions or more than two actions.

Incorrect Adverb Form	Correct Adverb Form
Lori jumped **highest** than Eva did. The team cheered **more excitedly** of all the teams at the race.	Lori jumped **higher** than Eva did. The team cheered **most excitedly** of all the teams at the race.

Connect Grammar to Writing

As you edit your fictional narrative, look closely at the adverbs you use. Correct any errors you notice. Using adverbs correctly is an important part of good writing.

W.3.3a establish a situation and introduce a narrator or characters/organize an event sequence; **W.3.3b** use dialogue and descriptions to develop experiences and events or show characters' responses; **W.3.3c** use temporal words and phrases to signal event order; **W.3.3d** provide a sense of closure

Narrative Writing

✔ **Ideas**   In **fictional narrative paragraphs,** good writers start by introducing a character or narrator and clearly establishing the setting. They tell events in a sequence that makes sense, and they finish with a good ending. Good writers also may use dialogue and descriptions to develop the story.

Holly wrote a scene about a wagon train. When she revised her draft, she added details and fixed the sequence.

Writing Traits Checklist

✔ **Ideas**
Did I establish a situation and introduce a narrator?

✔ **Organization**
Did I tell story events in a natural order?

✔ **Word Choice**
Did I use dialogue and description?

✔ **Voice**
Did I provide a strong ending?

✔ **Sentence Fluency**
Did I use different kinds of sentences?

✔ **Conventions**
Did I check my spelling?

Revised Draft

At one river crossing, we nearly lost our

wagon ∧ ~~The~~ oxen moved into the swift-
       when

flowing water. My mother jumped off the

wagon and waded quickly into the water.

Then one of them stumbled into a deep

spot. ∧ wagon would tip over.
      If the ox fell into the water, the

Next, she grabbed the rope around the

ox's neck.

232

Pioneer Mother

by Holly Becker

My mother wasn't afraid of much. After my father died on the Oregon Trail, she decided to keep going west instead of turning around. She drove our oxen confidently, or she tirelessly walked beside them. At one river crossing, we nearly lost our wagon when the oxen moved into the swift-flowing water. Then one of them stumbled into a deep spot. If the ox fell into the water, the wagon would tip over.

My mother jumped off the wagon and waded quickly into the water. Next, she grabbed the rope around the ox's neck. She pulled up and to the side. The struggling ox moved sideways and stepped into shallower water. "Let's go," she said as she moved forward and continued to lead the team. We made it safely across the river, and my mother never showed any fear!

Reading as a Writer

What details did Holly add to the beginning? How did she improve the sequence of events? What can you do to improve the sequence in your narrative paragraphs?

In my final paper, I added details to set the scene and changed the sequence to make it clearer.

Vocabulary in Context

migrate
survival
plenty
frightening
accidents
solid
chilly
landscape
thunderous
dramatic

Vocabulary Reader   Context Cards

L.3.6 acquire and use conversational, general academic, and domain-specific words and phrases

1 migrate
These butterflies fly far away when they migrate, or move from place to place.

2 survival
This bluebird flies south for the winter for its survival, or to stay alive.

3 plenty
Some animals don't migrate in winter if they have saved plenty of food.

4 frightening
It is frightening, or scary, for penguins when leopard seals come nearby.

Go Digital

▶ Study each Context Card.

▶ Use two Vocabulary words to tell about an experience you had.

⑤ accidents

When moose cross busy roads to find food, accidents can happen.

⑥ solid

It is very hard for animals to find food under snow and solid ice.

⑦ chilly

Polar bears have thick fur to keep them warm in cold, chilly weather.

⑧ landscape

The landscape changes in spring. Grass turns green, and flowers bloom.

⑨ thunderous

A herd of caribou makes a very loud, thunderous sound as it runs.

⑩ dramatic

Salmon swimming upstream to lay eggs is a dramatic, or exciting, sight.

235

Read and Comprehend

☑ TARGET SKILL

Compare and Contrast As you read *The Journey: Stories of Migration*, look for ways to **compare** and **contrast** important details about the two different kinds of migrating creatures. Note that the author uses a similar structure for both parts of the selection. This helps you see how the migrations are alike and different. Use a graphic organizer like this one to record text evidence that helps you compare and contrast the two migrations.

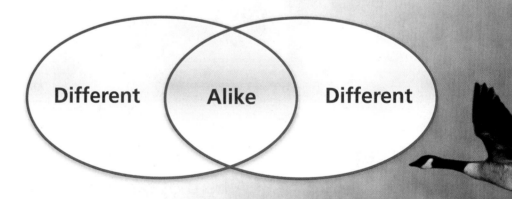

Different   Alike   Different

☑ TARGET STRATEGY

Visualize As you read, use the author's descriptive details to help you **visualize**, or picture, the information you read.

Animal Migration

Geese fly in a V-shape high in the sky. Hundreds of monarch butterflies gather on a tree trunk to rest during their long flight to Mexico. Sea turtles gather on Florida beaches in the spring and summer. These are just a few examples of migrations made every year. A migration is the movement of insects, animals, or even people from one location to another, often thousands of miles apart.

In *The Journey: Stories of Migration*, you'll learn why two very different creatures—gray whales and locusts—migrate and where they go.

ANCHOR TEXT

CYNTHIA RYLANT
The Journey
Stories of
Migration

illustrated by
LAMBERT DAVIS

✓ TARGET SKILL

Compare and Contrast
Tell how details are alike and different.

✓ GENRE

Informational text gives you facts and information about a topic. As you read, look for:

▸ headings that tell about the content of sections
▸ how the ideas and information are organized
▸ graphics such as maps to help explain the topic

COMMON CORE **RI.3.8** describe the connection between sentences and paragraphs in a text; **RI.3.10** read and comprehend informational texts; **L.3.3a** choose words and phrases for effect

MEET THE AUTHOR

Cynthia Rylant

What advice does an award-winning, famous author like Cynthia Rylant have for young writers? Go out and play. "Playing is still the greatest training you can have, I think, for being a writer," says Rylant. "It helps you love life, it helps you relax, and it helps you cook up interesting stuff in your head." She is the author of *The Blue Hill Meadows* and many other books.

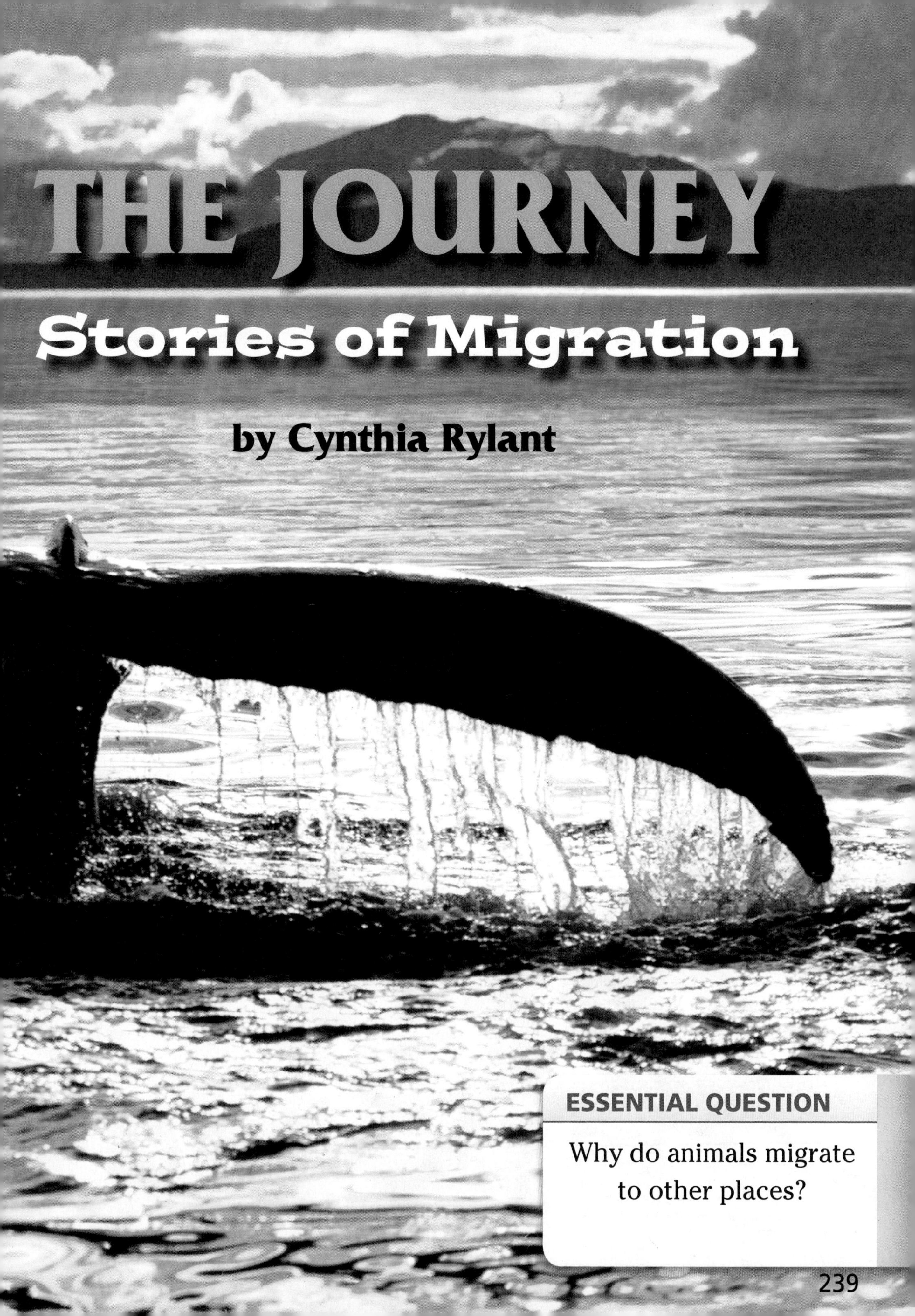

THE JOURNEY
Stories of Migration

by Cynthia Rylant

ESSENTIAL QUESTION

Why do animals migrate to other places?

Introduction

Most creatures live out their lives in the places where they are born. The tiny mouse runs in the fields where his mother ran. The gray squirrel lives in the same tall trees all her life. The cow stays on the farm.

But there are some creatures who do not stay where they are born, who cannot stay. These are the creatures who migrate. Their lives will be spent moving from one place to another. Some will migrate to survive. Some will migrate to create new life. All will be remarkable.

Here are the stories of two of these remarkable travelers—so different from each other but so alike in one profound way: Each must *move*.

The Locusts

There are few migrations as dramatic and frightening as when the desert locusts are moving across Africa. These insects are actually young grasshoppers, and grasshoppers usually do not travel.

But sometimes too many grasshopper eggs are laid in one small area, and when the grasshoppers are born, there isn't enough food. The grasshoppers now have only one choice for survival: to migrate in search of vegetation.

And so these grasshoppers will begin changing. Their bodies will turn from light green to dark yellow or red. Their antennae will grow short rather than long. And when they rise up to fly together by the *billions*, they will be grasshoppers no more. They will be locusts.

A cloud of desert locusts in the sky is an unbelievable sight. There are so many locusts that they block out the sun. It seems like night. And in the sudden darkness there is a terrible thunderous noise. It is the noise of a billion wings.

ANALYZE THE TEXT

Author's Word Choice What words help you visualize how it looks and sounds when the locusts fly away together?

What happens next is even more incredible. When the locusts fly to the ground, they will eat every plant, every blade of grass, every leaf and bush and piece of vegetation as far as the eye can see. Within minutes they will fly off again, leaving behind them a totally devastated landscape.

And though locusts do not willfully hurt people—they want only to eat gardens, trees, bushes, grass—people may die because of the locusts. Because the gardens are empty of food, people may die of starvation.

Desert locusts can also cause accidents. Locusts fly very high—as high as two miles up in the sky—and this can make difficult flying for planes that have to move through the locust cloud. The swarms can also interfere with trains. And millions of crushed locusts on a highway will make cars slip and slide.

There are many stories in history about the terrible devastation of locust plagues. It is written that in ancient times, one locust swarm covered 2,000 square miles.

The swarms today are not nearly as large as that. But they can still be quite big, often as much as one hundred square miles. Imagine so many insects in the sky!

locust eggs

As the locusts migrate in search of food, they ride the winds from one area of rainfall to the next. (There is always more food where it rains.) They travel on sunny mornings and stop in late afternoon to roost for the night.

When they reach a rainy area, they mate and die. Then their eggs will hatch and a new swarm of locusts begins moving. This will happen again and again until one day a swarm will return to the same place where the very first locusts began.

And if the eggs laid are not too many, and if there is plenty of food when the new eggs hatch, there will be no locust swarms for a while. Only pale green grasshoppers moving quietly about.

But someday too many eggs may be laid, and the newly hatched grasshoppers will be much too hungry. These grasshoppers will begin to look a little different and act a little different.

Then they will rise up together by the billions—as desert locusts—and they will fly.

The Whales

Many mammals migrate, but no mammal migrates as far as the big gray whale. It travels 6,000 miles, then back again—and most of its traveling is done on an empty stomach!

Gray whales love the cold waters near the North Pole because the waters are full of the food they love to eat. The whales live on tiny ocean shrimp and worms, and the Arctic waters are full of these in summer. The whales eat and eat and eat, straining the tiny food through strips of baleen in their mouths. (Instead of teeth, the grays have baleen—long strips of a hard material similar to fingernails.)

The gray whales swim and eat mostly alone through the summer. But in the fall, they will begin to look for some traveling companions, because the whales know one thing for certain: that they must migrate. In winter, the Arctic seas are going to be filled with solid ice. And the whales will die if they stay.

The first gray whales to leave the Arctic are the pregnant females. These expectant mothers want to have plenty of time to reach the warm waters of California and Mexico before they give birth. No mother wants to have a baby in icy water!

The other whales will follow, and in small groups they will all travel down the Pacific coast. Once they leave the Arctic, the whales won't find much food again, and it may be as long as *eight months* before they eat.

But the whales have stored a lot of fat in their bodies, called blubber, and this will keep them alive.

As they travel, the whales often swim near shore, and people along the way are thrilled. They wave to the whales from rocky cliffs and travel out in boats to say hello to them.

When finally the gray whales reach the warm tropical waters in January, the pregnant females will give birth. And the other whales will mate.

With new calves among them, all of the whales will enjoy life in the peaceful lagoons for a while. Then in March, they will be ready to head back to the Arctic for the summer. They haven't forgotten how they love to eat there!

This time the males will leave first, and the females and calves will stay behind for another several weeks. The calves will have more time to grow and get stronger for the long journey.

The arrows on the map show the gray whales' 6,000-mile journey from the Arctic, then back again.

Finally, all of the whales will travel, up past Oregon, past Washington, through the waters of Alaska and Asia, up near the North Pole. How do the whales find these Arctic waters? No one is sure. The whales might follow the shape of the ocean beds. They might sense the earth's magnetic field, like living compasses. They may use echolocation—sending out sounds which bounce back and describe what is all around.

But somehow the whales will travel that long 6,000-mile journey north, and they will find the same chilly waters they left behind. When they arrive in the Arctic, they will separate and enjoy a summer of fine ocean eating.

ANALYZE THE TEXT

Compare and Contrast What is the same about the two trips that whales make? What is different?

But just before the Arctic winter arrives, before the ice, something will tell the whales to find each other again. To find some company for another long, long swim.

Dig Deeper

How to Analyze the Text

Use these pages to learn about Comparing and Contrasting and Author's Word Choice. Then read *The Journey: Stories of Migration* again to apply what you learned.

Compare and Contrast

The author of *The Journey: Stories of Migration* organized the text in a way that helps readers **compare** and **contrast** whales and locusts. Looking for connections between parts of a text will help you understand what you read.

Return to pages 240 and 241 in *The Journey: Stories of Migration*. First, you will learn that some animals migrate while others do not. Then you will start reading about one migratory animal, the locust. As you continue reading, look for text evidence that helps you make connections. When you come to the next section, about whales, you will be able to start comparing and contrasting the information with what you read about locusts.

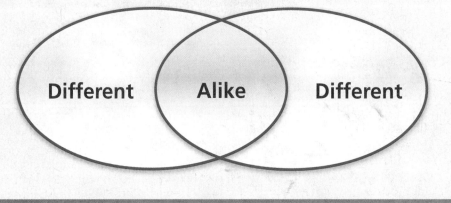

RI.3.8 describe the connection between sentences and paragraphs in a text; **L.3.3a** choose words and phrases for effect

Author's Word Choice

Authors carefully choose the words and phrases they use. Choosing strong **adjectives** and **adverbs** helps readers picture what things look like and how events happen.

In *The Journey: Stories of Migration*, the author uses the words *dramatic and frightening* to describe a swarm of locusts on page 241. Think about how those words help you imagine the young grasshoppers.

Your Turn

Review the selection with a partner to prepare to discuss this question: *Why do animals migrate to other places?* As you use text evidence to discuss the question, listen carefully to your partner's ideas and expand the discussion by adding your own ideas.

Classroom Conversation

Continue your discussion of *The Journey: Stories of Migration* by explaining your answers to these questions:

1. How do people feel about locust migration? Whale migration? How do these feelings differ?

2. There are a few ideas about how gray whales know where to go. Which makes the most sense to you?

3. How would you describe these migrations to someone who has not read the selection?

WRITE ABOUT READING

Response Think about the two migrations in *The Journey: Stories of Migration*. If you could watch either the locusts migrate or the whales migrate, which would you choose? Write a paragraph about your choice. Use text evidence from the selection to support your opinion.

Writing Tip

As you write, choose words and phrases that emphasize your point of view. Use adjectives that help readers visualize what you describe.

COMMON CORE **RI.3.1** ask and answer questions to demonstrate understanding, referring to the text; **W.3.10** write routinely over extended time frames or short time frames; **SL.3.1a** come to discussions prepared/explicitly draw on preparation and other information about the topic; **SL.3.1d** explain own ideas and understanding in light of the discussion; **L.3.3a** choose words and phrases for effect

FABLE

The Grasshopper and the Ant

an **Aesop's fable** adapted by **Margaretha Rabe**

Grasshopper loved to sing and play his fiddle. He played quiet songs and thunderous tunes. Sometimes Grasshopper played frightening music. Then he would hop around in a dramatic way. That's when he caused accidents.

One time Grasshopper jumped into a pile of grain that Ant had spent all day collecting. The grain scattered across the landscape.

RL.3.2 recount stories and determine the message, lesson, or moral; **RL.3.10** read and comprehend literature

"You should be more careful, Grasshopper," scolded Ant. "I worked hard to gather that grain. Now I have to pile it up again."

"I'm sorry," said Grasshopper. "Why not take a break? It's a beautiful, sunny day. You'll have plenty of days to gather food."

"You may think so, Grasshopper, but winter will soon be here. Then the ground will be frozen solid," said Ant. "Now is the time to gather food and plan for survival. You should take a break from playing and do some work."

Grasshopper said, "I'll migrate to someplace warm if it gets too chilly. That way, I can keep on playing and singing. But for now I'll play any song you like to make your work easier to do."

Weeks later, fat flakes of snow began to drift from the sky. Grasshopper shivered. It was so cold that he could hardly hold his fiddle. Grasshopper looked for food, but the ground had turned into a blanket of white snow.

"What will I do now? I can't find food, and it's too cold for me to go far. Maybe Ant will help me," thought Grasshopper.

Grasshopper trudged through the snow and knocked on Ant's door. "Will you give me food if I sing and play for you?" asked Grasshopper.

Ant said, "Yes I will. I worked hard the rest of the year, so now I have time to relax and have fun."

Moral: There are times to work and times to play.

Compare Texts

Compare Grasshoppers Compare and contrast the grasshoppers in the two selections. What problem do the grasshoppers share in both selections? What do they do about this problem? Use text evidence to make a list of how the grasshoppers are alike and different.

Grasshopper or Ant? In *The Grasshopper and the Ant*, Grasshopper likes to play, and Ant is always working. Are you more like Grasshopper or Ant? Are you a little bit like both? Write a paragraph explaining your answer and giving examples.

Moral of the Story With a partner, reread *Two Bear Cubs* from Lesson 19. Review the play's moral or message. How is it like the moral of *The Grasshopper and the Ant*? How is it different? Explain how the morals can apply to real life.

Go Digital

COMMON CORE **RL.3.1** ask and answer questions to demonstrate understanding, referring to the text; **RL.3.2** recount stories and determine the message, lesson or moral; **RI.3.1** ask and answer questions to demonstrate understanding, referring to the text; **RI.3.9** compare and contrast important points and details in texts on the same topic

Grammar

Making Comparisons Adjectives are used to describe nouns. They can also be used to **compare nouns.**

• Add -*er* to most adjectives to compare two nouns.

• Add -*est* to most adjectives to compare more than two.

Adverbs tell when, where, or how something happened. They can also be used to **compare actions.**

• Add -*er* to many adverbs to compare two actions.

• Add -*est* to many adverbs to compare more than two actions.

Adjective	Adverb
Ben is tall.	Jen can jump high.
Ben is taller than Jack.	I can jump higher than Jen.
Ben is the tallest boy in class.	Cho can jump highest of all.

Try This! **Copy each sentence. Fill in the blank with the correct form of the adjective or adverb in parentheses.**

1. The _____ whale swam ahead of the other whales. (large)

2. Mr. Briggs sang _____ than the music teacher. (soft)

3. This test is the _____ we have had so far. (hard)

4. Abby ran _____ of all the runners in the race. (fast)

When you write a descriptive paragraph, you can make comparisons to describe what something looks like or how it moves. Comparisons will help readers clearly imagine your ideas.

Adjective	Adverb
A blue whale is large.	A gray whale dives deep.
A blue whale is larger than an elephant.	A gray whale dives deeper than a blue whale.
Blue whales are the largest animals on Earth.	Sperm whales dive deepest of all whales.

Connect Grammar to Writing

As you revise your descriptive paragraph, look for ways to use adjectives and adverbs to compare. Be sure to use the correct form to show how many things or actions are being compared.

Narrative Writing

Word Choice ✔ In *The Journey: Stories of Migration,* you read that a billion locusts' wings sound like thunder. *Like thunder* is a simile. It is a phrase that uses *like* or *as* to compare two things. That is one way to help your readers picture what you describe.

Victor wrote a **descriptive paragraph** about a whale-watching trip. He revised his draft by adding a simile and strong descriptive words.

Writing Traits Checklist

✔ **Ideas**
Did I state my topic clearly?

✔ **Organization**
Are my ideas in an order that makes sense?

✔ **Word Choice**
Did I use sensory details?

✔ **Voice**
Did I use similes to describe what something felt like?

✔ **Sentence Fluency**
Did I use phrases that tell where and when?

✔ **Conventions**
Did I edit my work for spelling, grammar, and punctuation?

Revised Draft

When we finally spotted a whale, I was shocked. It was just floating , looking like an island. It didn't look like a whale. Then the island dove into the ocean! In seconds, the whale popped up again. Then the whale leaped high out of the ocean, showering us with chilly seawater. As the whale dove quickly back into the waves, it flapped its huge, fanlike tail. That tail was bigger than our boat.

My Whale-Watching Trip
by Victor Rotello

Mom and I took a whale-watching trip last summer. At first, it seemed to be an ocean-watching trip. When we finally spotted a whale, I was shocked. It was just floating, looking like an island. It didn't look like a whale. Then the island dove into the ocean! In seconds, the whale popped up again. Then the whale leaped high out of the ocean, showering us with chilly seawater. As the whale dove quickly back into the waves, it flapped its huge, fanlike tail. That tail was bigger than our boat. "Bye!" I yelled as I waved, feeling like I was saying goodbye to an old friend. Mom and I had seen what we came for, a giant whale. What a great trip!

Reading as a Writer

Victor added a simile to describe his first look at the whale. What similes could you use in your descriptive paragraph?

In my final paragraph, I added a simile and adjectives to describe what things looked and felt like.

Vocabulary in Context

☑ **TARGET VOCABULARY**

sincere
managed
loaded
loveliest
conversations
inspired
reunion
currently
pleasure
terror

Vocabulary Reader   Context Cards

Route 66

L.3.6 acquire and use conversational, general academic, and domain-specific words and phrases

COMMON CORE

1 **sincere**
This President had sincere hopes. He truly wanted to change unfair laws.

2 **managed**
Artists managed to carve this special monument. It was not easy!

3 **loaded**
Before sailing, people loaded onto this swan boat. They piled on.

4 **loveliest**
Oregon's Crater Lake is one of the loveliest national parks. It is beautiful.

 Go Digital

▶ Study each Context Card.

▶ Place the Vocabulary words in alphabetical order.

⑤ conversations

Conversations in a museum must be quiet. People should speak in whispers.

⑥ inspired

This statue has inspired people. It makes them believe in freedom.

⑦ reunion

This family went camping for their yearly reunion, or gathering.

⑧ currently

Currently, this fort is a museum. Soldiers no longer live here.

⑨ pleasure

People get pleasure, or enjoyment, from riding this old merry-go-round.

⑩ terror

When people look down at the Grand Canyon, they may feel terror, or fear.

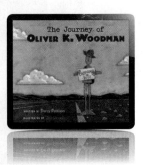

Read and Comprehend

 Go Digital

Sequence of Events As you read *The Journey of Oliver K. Woodman*, note the **sequence**, or order, in which things happen in the story. Clues such as dates, time of day, and signal words can help you determine the sequence. Use a chart like this one to record the events in sequence. The chart can help you describe how each event builds on earlier parts of the story.

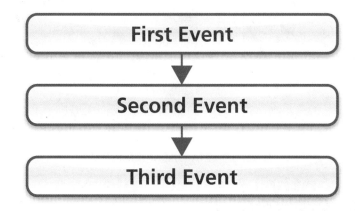

First Event

↓

Second Event

↓

Third Event

✓ TARGET STRATEGY

Analyze/Evaluate As you read *The Journey of Oliver K. Woodman*, pay attention to how the author chooses to tell Oliver's story. Use text evidence to **analyze** and **evaluate** whether or not you think this works well.

Sending Messages

Think of all the ways people communicate today. People send messages in many ways, including e-mails, letters and postcards, and text messages. Even smiling and waving at another person are ways to communicate.

Most animals send messages to each other, too. Birds call to each other. Dogs bark warnings and wag their tails to say hello.

The Journey of Oliver K. Woodman tells the story of how people help the strangely quiet Oliver K. Woodman send messages in interesting and amusing ways.

ANCHOR TEXT

The Journey of
OLIVER K. WOODMAN

WRITTEN BY Darcy Pattison
ILLUSTRATED BY

☑ TARGET SKILL

Sequence of Events Tell the time order in which events happen.

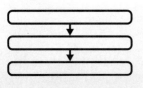

☑ GENRE

A **fantasy** is an imaginative story that could not happen in real life. As you read, look for:
▶ story events or settings that are not realistic
▶ characters that act in ways that are not real

MEET THE AUTHOR
Darcy Pattison

Oliver K. Woodman, the character Darcy Pattison created, has become so popular that students at schools in New York, Indiana, and other states have their own wooden models of him. Whenever they travel, they take Oliver with them and bring back photos and journal entries from his journey.

MEET THE ILLUSTRATOR
Joe Cepeda

Joe Cepeda does woodworking as a hobby, so when he was illustrating this story, he drew Oliver K. Woodman as if he were really going to build the character out of wood. Author Darcy Pattison loves how Cepeda's art turned out. "Oliver has no mouth, yet you would swear that he's smiling at us," she says.

COMMON CORE **RL.3.5** refer to parts of stories, dramas, and poems/describe how each part builds on earlier sections; **RL.3.10** read and comprehend literature; **L.3.3b** recognize and observe differences between conventions of spoken and written standard English

THE JOURNEY OF OLIVER K. WOODMAN

written by
Darcy Pattison

illustrated by
Joe Cepeda

ESSENTIAL QUESTION

How can people
communicate over
long distances?

May 10
Redcrest, CA

Dear Uncle Ray,
    Please come to visit us this summer.
We will go camping. We can swim and
catch fish.
    You are my favorite uncle. Please say
you will come!

                                Love,
                                Tameka
                                XOXOXO

May 17
Rock Hill, SC

Dear Tameka,

I'd love to come to California, but I can't.
I will be building kitchen cabinets for some new
apartments all summer.

But maybe my friend Oliver will come to visit!

Love,
Uncle Ray

ANALYZE THE TEXT

Sequence of Events Who wrote the first letter, Uncle Ray or Tameka? How can you figure this out?

Dear Traveler,

I am going to see Tameka Schwartz,
370 Park Avenue, Redcrest, California, 95569.
Please give me a ride and help me get there.
If you don't mind, drop a note to my friend
Raymond Johnson, 111 Stony Lane, Rock Hill,
South Carolina, 29730. He wants to keep up
with my travels.

Thanks,
Oliver K. Woodman

June 1
Rock Hill, SC

Dear Favorite Niece Tameka,
    Oliver left this morning. Let me know when
he gets there—it should take him a couple of
weeks. Or maybe more. It's hard to say.

Love,
Uncle Ray

June 4
McTavish Plantation
Outside Memphis, Tennessee

Dear Ray:
    For two days, Oliver rode in the back of my truck and kept Bert, my Brahman bull, company. I delivered Bert to his new home and he's settling in, but he'll miss the late-night conversations and singing with Oliver.
    I left Oliver east of the Mississippi River, just outside Memphis, and hurried home to my beloved Amelia.

                    Yours truly,
                    Jackson McTavish

June 8
Forrest City, AR

Hi! Mr. OK is OK. Quinn and Sherry went to a basketball game at The Pyramid in Memphis, Tennessee, last weekend and brought Mr. OK back. He hung out with us for a couple of days, and all the girls liked him better than Quinn. So when Quinn's cousin's boyfriend's aunt was leaving to visit her sick grandfather in Fort Smith, Arkansas, the guys loaded Mr. OK into the aunt's station wagon and sent him on his way. We didn't even get to say good-bye!

Cherry (Sherry's sister),
for the Gang

P.S. If you see Mr. OK again, tell him we all said good-bye.

Raymond Johnson
111 Stony Lane
Rock Hill, SC 29730

ANALYZE THE TEXT

Formal and Informal Language How does Cherry's letter sound different from Jackson's letter on page 279? Which words make it sound this way?

281

June 11
Albuquerque, NM

Hey, Ray—
  I drive a moving van for Southeast Moving Company. I picked up Oliver at the Arkansas border, then drove west to Oklahoma City, Oklahoma, south to Dallas, Texas, northwest to Amarillo, Texas, east to Panhandle, Texas, then west again to Albuquerque, New Mexico.
  He's an easy fella to travel with. He never needs bathroom stops. He doesn't care where we eat. And he stays awake with me all night. I'm sorry to see him go, but this week the company is sending me east, to Wauchula, Florida.
                    Trucking along—
                    Bobbi Jo

Raymond Johnson
111 Stony Lane
Rock Hill, SC 29730

June 28
Rock Hill, SC

Dear Tameka,

I've had no word from Oliver in seventeen days. I'm starting to worry. What if he is lost? Please call me if he turns up at your house.

Love,
Uncle Ray

July 1
Redcrest, CA

Dear Uncle Ray,

No word from Oliver. Are you sure he's really coming?

I still wish we could see you. I asked Mama if we could come visit, but she said it costs too much. Daddy says he can't take off work that long. Ever since I asked, Mama keeps looking at family photo albums. When she sees your pictures, she says, "My baby brother!"

Love,
Tameka
XOXOXOX

July 4
Salt Lake City, UT

Dear Raymond Johnson:
My grandfather found Mr. Woodman in the middle of the reservation in New Mexico. Poor fella—a mouse was building a nest in his backpack. We don't know how he ended up way out there, and he's not telling.
Grandpa brought him to Utah to join me in the Fourth of July parade. I got so tired of smiling and waving at the crowds, but Mr. Woodman's brave smile inspired me.
I just sent Mr. Woodman off with three sisters. They looked like such nice old ladies, so I know they'll take good care of him.

With all my love—
Melissa Tso, Miss Utah

P.S. I've enclosed an autographed picture.

July 27
en route to San Francisco, CA

Dear Mr. Johnson:

My sisters and I had the distinct pleasure of entertaining Mr. Oliver K. Woodman for the past 23 days.

You see, we've lived in Kokomo, Indiana, all our lives. Until now, we'd never been west of the Mississippi River. Our dear papa died in January and left us an inheritance. We decided to use the money to tour the West this year.

While in Salt Lake City, we saw Mr. Oliver in a parade, and after talking it over, we voted to give him a ride. We stopped at a rodeo in Eureka, Nevada, where Mr. Oliver met an old friend named Bert. They had a moving reunion.

We are heading south to San Francisco to see the Golden Gate Bridge, so we left Mr. Oliver yesterday in Rough and Ready, California. He should be at Miss Tameka's soon.

The Claremont Sisters
Agnes, Maggie, and Lucinda

P.S. We had afternoon tea every day. Mr. Oliver has the loveliest manners.

July 28
To: Raymond Johnson
Re: Mr. Oliver K. Woodman

Our family, currently on vacation, picked up the above-named person in what I thought was a misguided goodwill gesture. Little did I know how lucky that gesture would be.

Last night, we pitched tents in the Redwood forest. I woke at 3:00 A.M. to screams of terror. Bears! Your friend managed to frighten them away. He saved our lives.

With the deepest and most sincere gratitude, we intend to deliver him to the doorstep of Tameka Schwartz within the next two days.

Gratefully yours,
Bernard Grape,
Attorney-at-Law

Raymond Johnson
111 Stony Lane
Rock Hill, SC
29730

August 1
Redcrest, CA

Dear Uncle Ray,

Guess who came to dinner? Oliver!

He is so much fun! We are camping in the backyard tonight. I hear he's not scared of anything, so I'm glad he'll be there. Tomorrow, at the river, I'll let him hold my fishing pole while I swim.

Guess what else? Daddy and Mama talked it over. We're coming to your house next month, and we'll bring Oliver home. Isn't it wonderful?

Love,
Tameka
XOXOXOX

P.S. Knock, knock. Who's there? Olive. Olive who? Olive both you and Oliver!

Oliver's Journey

TICKER-TAPE PARADE FOR HOMETOWN BOY

by Demetrius Dickson

Oliver K. Woodman will return home today amid national acclaim for his cross-country journey. Woodman began his trip on June 1, in Rock Hill, South Carolina, and arrived in Redcrest, California, on August 1.

The Rock Hill City Council announced that a ticker-tape parade to honor Woodman will be held today at 10:00 A.M., starting at the corner of Main Street and Cherry Road and proceeding down Cherry Road to Cherry Park.

Raymond Johnson and Tameka Schwartz, friends of Mr. Woodman, will host a picnic in his honor at Cherry Park at noon. At 1:00 P.M., Mr. Woodman will show postcards and mementos from his trip. The public is invited.

Dig Deeper

How to Analyze the Text

Use these pages to learn about Sequence of Events and Formal and Informal Language. Then read *The Journey of Oliver K. Woodman* again to apply what you learned.

Sequence of Events

The order in which things happen in a story is called the **sequence of events**. Stories often have clues to help readers follow the sequence. At times, the clues are words such as *first*, *next*, and *last*. In *The Journey of Oliver K. Woodman*, the clues are the dates at the top of each letter.

The chart below shows a way to keep track of the sequence of events in the story. You can use the completed chart to guide you back to parts of the story. It can also help you describe how each event builds on earlier parts of the story.

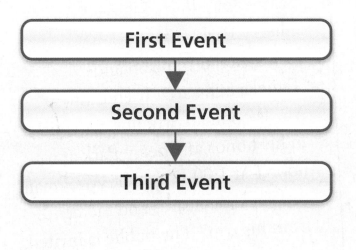

First Event

↓

Second Event

↓

Third Event

RL.3.5 refer to parts of stories, dramas, and poems/describe how each part builds on earlier sections; **L.3.3b** recognize and observe differences between conventions of spoken and written standard English

Formal and Informal Language

Formal language sounds serious and polite. The words are exact and carefully chosen. **Informal language** sounds more relaxed. It is how friends talk to each other.

Written language can be formal or informal. In *The Journey of Oliver K. Woodman*, some of the letters are informal and sound like people speaking. Some examples are words like *hung out, the guys*, and *poor fella*. Other letters use more formal language, such as *distinct pleasure*.

Your Turn

Turn and Talk Review the story with a partner to prepare to discuss this question: *How can people communicate over long distances?* In your discussion, talk about your own experience as well as text evidence from the selection.

Classroom Conversation

Now talk about these questions with the class:

1 Does seeing the sequence of events make the story easier or harder for you to follow? Explain your answer.

2 How do the illustrations give you more information about Oliver?

3 How does Oliver K. Woodman help Uncle Ray and Tameka communicate?

WRITE ABOUT READING

Response Think about what happens when Oliver scares away bears in the Redwood forest. What would Oliver say if he had a voice? Write a letter from Oliver that explains how you got there and what happened when you saw the bears.

The Journey of OLIVER K. WOODMAN

WRITTEN BY Darcy Pattison
ILLUSTRATED BY Joe Cepeda

Writing Tip

As you write your letter, use colorful adjectives and action verbs to describe where you are and what happens.

COMMON CORE **RL.3.1** ask and answer questions to demonstrate understanding, referring to the text; **RL.3.5** refer to parts of stories, dramas, and poems/describe how each part builds on earlier sections; **RL.3.7** explain how illustrations contribute to the words; **W.3.10** write routinely over extended time frames or short time frames; **SL.3.1a** come to discussions prepared/explicitly draw on preparation and other information about the topic; **SL.3.1d** explain own ideas and understanding in light of the discussion; **L.3.1d** form and use regular and irregular verbs; **L.3.3a** choose words and phrases for effect

INFORMATIONAL TEXT

Moving the U.S. Mail

✓ GENRE

Informational text gives factual information about a topic. This is an online encyclopedia.

✓ TEXT FOCUS

A **timeline** is a line that shows the order in which events happened.

Moving the U.S. Mail

The United States Postal Service

The United States Postal Service has changed over the years. In colonial times, all kinds of people helped deliver mail. Sometimes letters managed to get through. Sometimes they didn't.

Delivery Times
New York to San Francisco

1800

Pony Express 13–14 days by train to Missouri, then on horseback

COMMON CORE **RI.3.7** use information gained from illustrations and words to demonstrate understanding; **RI.3.10** read and comprehend informational texts

Getting mail brings pleasure to many, but it has never been easy to deliver. Today the Postal Service makes a sincere effort to deliver all mail. Currently it delivers hundreds of millions of messages daily.

Transportation Changes

Having conversations by mail has gotten much faster. Why is this? Transportation has improved. Long ago, people carried mail on foot, horseback, and stagecoaches. Today's mail is loaded onto trucks and planes.

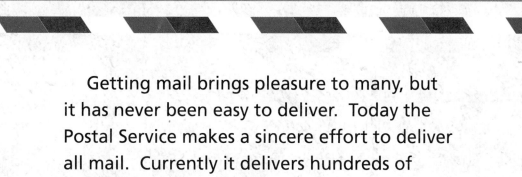

In 1775 Benjamin Franklin became the first Postmaster General.

1900   2000

Transcontinental Railroad 7 days

Airplane 6–7 hours

Golden Moments of Mail History

Gold was discovered in California in 1848. People rushed west. The California Gold Rush inspired faster mail delivery. It would be a long time until they could have a reunion with their families, so gold seekers wanted mail from home.

Pony Express riders carried mail to California in 1860 and 1861. Their rides could be full of terror. They faced blizzards and bandits.

By 1869 the Transcontinental Railroad linked railroads in the east with California. The mail moved faster than ever.

A Postmark from the Heart

Each year around February 14, mail from around the world takes a detour. This mail isn't slowed by blizzards or bandits—it's delayed by love! In honor of Valentine's Day, cards are mailed to the small town of Valentine, Texas. They get the town's postmark and go on to their final destination.

Each year, in Valentine, Texas, the school holds a design contest. The city council chooses the loveliest design to be used as that year's postmark.

Aunt Susie
123 Msososo Street
Austin, TX 12307

Compare Texts

TEXT TO TEXT

Compare Mail Delivery Think about what it would have been like if Oliver K. Woodman had traveled to California by Pony Express. How would his trip be the same or different? Use text evidence from *Moving the U.S. Mail* to write a paragraph describing Oliver K. Woodman's trip by Pony Express.

TEXT TO SELF

Write a Letter What would you do with Oliver K. Woodman if he visited you? Write a letter to Uncle Ray about the adventures you would have. Include a date, a greeting, and a closing. Use friendly, informal language.

TEXT TO WORLD

Connect to Social Studies Use a road map of the United States to find the places that Oliver K. Woodman visits. Identify the general direction in which he traveled. Give a brief report to a group of classmates, telling them what you learned.

COMMON CORE **RI.3.1** ask and answer questions to demonstrate understanding, referring to the text; **W.3.10** write routinely over extended time frames or short time frames; **SL.3.1a** come to discussions prepared/explicitly draw on preparation and other information about the topic; **SL.3.4** report on a topic or text, tell a story, or recount an experience/speak clearly at an understandable pace

303

Grammar

Possessive Nouns and Pronouns A **possessive noun** shows that a person or animal owns or has something. Add an apostrophe and *s* to make a singular or plural noun possessive. Add only an apostrophe to a plural noun that ends in *s*.

A **possessive pronoun** can take the place of a possessive noun to show who or what owns something.

Singular Possessive Noun	Plural Possessive Noun	Possessive Pronoun
boy's dog's	children's girls'	Singular: her, his, my, mine Plural: our, ours, their, theirs
boy's bike dog's toys	children's games girls' jackets	my bike our books

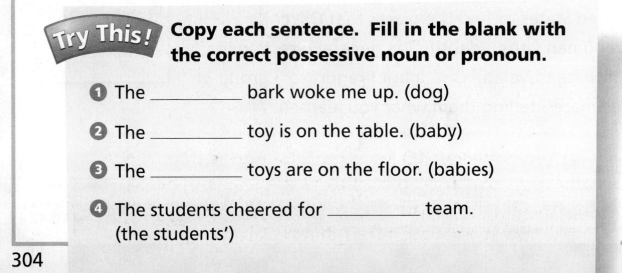

Try This! **Copy each sentence. Fill in the blank with the correct possessive noun or pronoun.**

1. The _____ bark woke me up. (dog)

2. The _____ toy is on the table. (baby)

3. The _____ toys are on the floor. (babies)

4. The students cheered for _____ team. (the students')

Good writers use possessive pronouns to avoid repeating possessive nouns and to make sentences smoother. Be sure to replace a singular or plural possessive noun with a singular or plural possessive pronoun.

Awkward Sentences	Smoother Sentences
The family's best outing was the family's trip to the zoo.	The family's best outing was their trip to the zoo.
Maria showed pictures to Maria's friends.	Maria showed pictures to her friends.
"The picture of the alligator is Maria's favorite," she said.	"The picture of the alligator is my favorite," she said.

Connect Grammar to Writing

As you write your dialogue, look for possessive nouns that you have repeated. Replace these nouns with possessive pronouns. Check that possessive pronouns match the possessive nouns they replace.

Narrative Writing

☑ **Voice** In *The Journey of Oliver K. Woodman*, you can tell how Tameka feels when she says in a letter, "You are my favorite uncle. Please say you will come!" As you revise your **dialogue**, be sure your characters speak in a way that shows their feelings.

Ava wrote about two girls who find a cave. When Ava revised her draft, her changes showed the girls' feelings.

Writing Traits Checklist

☑ **Ideas**
Is my dialogue interesting?

☑ **Organization**
Can my readers tell what is happening?

☑ **Word Choice**
Did I use formal or informal words that suit my characters?

☑ **Voice**
Do my characters' feelings show?

☑ **Sentence Fluency**
Did I use different kinds of sentences?

☑ **Conventions**
Did I indent each paragraph?

Revised Draft

Mia and Jade were exploring the woods behind their new house. "~~I found~~ ^Hey, look at this!" whispered ~~something,~~ ^said Mia.

"~~It's~~ ^Wow, a cave ^!" said Jade. "Let's go in."

"Are you kidding?"
^~~No, I don't want to.~~

"Why not?"

"There could be bears in there!"

Jade smiled. "~~I don't think so.~~ ^Don't be silly. Mrs. Chen said there are no bears around here."

The Cave

by Ava Garcia

Mia and Jade were exploring the woods behind their new house. "Hey, look at this!" whispered Mia.

"Wow, a cave!" said Jade. "Let's go in."

"Are you kidding?"

"Why not?"

"There could be bears in there!"

Jade smiled. "Don't be silly. Mrs. Chen said there are no bears around here."

Mia said, "Well, I have a cold, and Dr. Davis says damp places are bad for colds."

"You're just scared. I'm going in. I bet there's something fantastic in there."

"Well…okay. Let's go," said Mia.

The two girls took a few steps into the dark cave. There was a flutter of wings as a dozen bats flew out above the girls' heads. Jade screamed and ran back out.

"Haha! Now we know who is scared!" said Mia.

Reading as a Writer

Which parts let you really hear how each girl feels? Where can you show your own characters' feelings more clearly?

I added words that show my characters' feelings. I also made sure to write abbreviations correctly.

✓ TARGET VOCABULARY

voyage
lava
rippled
arrival
guided
twisted
aboard
anchor
spotted
bay

Vocabulary Reader	Context Cards

COMMON CORE **L.3.6** acquire and use conversational, general academic, and domain-specific words and phrases

Vocabulary in Context

1 voyage
The explorer's voyage, or ocean trip, to Hawaii took more than a year.

2 lava
Hawaii's islands formed from lava, or hot melted rock from volcanoes.

3 rippled
This lava in Hawaii rippled into tiny black waves as it cooled.

4 arrival
When visitors first come to Hawaii, their arrival is welcomed.

Go Digital

▶ Study each Context Card.

▶ Tell a story about two or more pictures, using the Vocabulary words.

---

5 guided

This man guided, or led, tourists through a park in Hawaii.

---

6 twisted

These girls twisted wire around flowers to attach them to crowns.

---

7 aboard

Each racing canoe has six people aboard. They are seated in the boat.

---

8 anchor

A heavy anchor holds this boat in place when the boat is stopped.

---

9 spotted

The tourists spotted, or caught sight of, whales in the ocean near Hawaii.

---

10 bay

People can swim, snorkel, or sail in the gentle waters of this bay, or inlet.

Read and Comprehend

✓ TARGET SKILL

Author's Purpose As you read *Dog-of-the-Sea-Waves*, think about how the author describes Hawaii. Write details and text evidence in a chart like the one below. Then use the information to help you figure out the **author's purpose,** or reason, for writing the story.

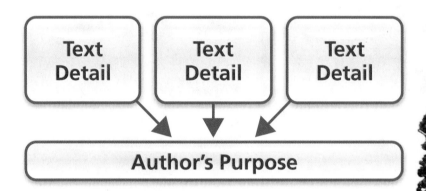

Text Detail	Text Detail	Text Detail

Author's Purpose

✓ TARGET STRATEGY

Question As you read, ask yourself **questions** about the text if there is something that you do not understand. Use text evidence to help you answer your questions.

Volcanoes

The Hawaiian Islands are lush, green, and beautiful. It is hard to believe that they were formed from red-hot bubbling rock rising from deep inside the earth. When the melted rock cooled, it hardened into land and formed islands. Plants such as palms and animals such as seals found their way to the islands. Eventually, people did, too.

In *Dog-of-the-Sea-Waves*, you'll read a story of five young men who explored these volcanic islands long ago. You'll find out what happens when one of the volcanoes wakens from its rest.

ANCHOR TEXT

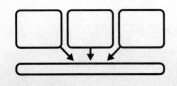

☑ TARGET SKILL

Author's Purpose Use text details to figure out why an author writes a selection.

☑ GENRE

Realistic fiction is a story that could happen in real life. As you read, look for:

▶ realistic characters and events
▶ a plot with a beginning, a middle, and an ending
▶ details that help the reader picture the setting

COMMON CORE **RL.3.1** ask and answer questions to demonstrate understanding, referring to the text; **RL.3.7** explain how illustrations contribute to the words; **RL.3.10** read and comprehend literature

Go Digital

MEET THE AUTHOR AND ILLUSTRATOR

James Rumford

A longtime resident of Hawaii, James Rumford hopes his readers will learn *aloha 'āina*, or "to cherish these islands," as much as he does. Scattered throughout the pages of *Dog-of-the-Sea-Waves* are drawings of plants and animals that are found in Hawaii. Many of them are at risk of dying out. Rumford included these to show that Hawaii's natural beauty needs our protection.

Dog-of-the-Sea-Waves

By James Rumford

ESSENTIAL QUESTION

What changes do volcanoes cause?

Five brothers explore the Hawaiian Islands. Manu, the youngest brother, saves the life of an injured seal and the two become friends. When it's time for the brothers to go home, Manu is unsure if he'll ever see his friend again.

O'ahu Tree Snail

In the days when the sun, the moon, and the stars guided birds with seeds in their bellies to these islands, when ocean waves brought driftwood teeming with life, when storms brought frightened birds in the clouds and insects on the wind, the Hawaiian Islands grew green and lush.

The streams and lagoons rippled with fish. And the forests flashed with the feathers of birds and the rainbow wings of insects.

Belted Wrasse

The Hawaiian Islands welcomed all life that made the long, long journey to its shores, and some two thousand years ago, they embraced the first people to come.

In those days of first canoes, first footprints, first campfires, there were five brothers who came from their home far to the south to explore these islands. They were Hōkū, who loved the stars, Nāʻale, who loved the sea, ʻŌpua, who loved clouds, Makani, who loved the wind, and Manu, who loved birds.

Kamehameha Butterfly

One night, soon after their arrival, Hōkū said, "See, my brothers, that new star I've discovered? It always points north!"

Everyone except Manu looked up at the sparkling North Star. Everyone except Manu began talking excitedly about all the other new things they had discovered.

"New things!" Manu exclaimed. "I miss the old things. Where are the coconuts, the bananas, the sweet potatoes? And how about the pigs, the chickens, the dogs?"

"We'll go home and bring these things back here with us," said Hōkū.

"We're coming back?" Manu cried. "I don't want to come back. I just want to go home."

But home was a long ocean voyage away, and there was much to do before they could leave—food and water to gather and sails to repair. So no one spoke.

The next day, as the brothers were exploring a lagoon, Manu spotted an animal lying at the water's edge.

"It's a dog, my brothers! A dog!"

At last! Something familiar in this strange land.

But when they got close, they saw that it was like no dog they had ever seen before. It had flippers for legs, a fish's tail, and the body of a dolphin. And it was badly hurt.

Manu tried to calm the animal. He brought cool water and cleaned the wound. He built a shelter against the sun and kept the fur wet with seawater.

The brothers left Manu. They had no time for an animal that was going to die. They had to prepare for the long sea voyage home.

But the animal didn't die.

"I will call you 'Dog-of-the-Sea-Waves,'" Manu said on the third day, as he fed him fish.

At the end of the week, the two had their first swim together, and before long, they were playing tag in the waves. Manu made up a silly chant:

Dog-of-the-Sea-Waves,
Dog-with-no-paws,
Dog-with-no-ears,
Dog-with-no-wag,
We're friends!

Granulated Cowry

Manu giggled, and Dog-of-the-Sea-Waves tickled his cheek with his whiskers.

"Come help me dry berries and roots for the voyage home," called Hōkū.

"We need fish," scolded Nāʻale.

"There's water to gather," scowled ʻŌpua.

"And sails to repair," cried Makani.

But Manu pretended not to hear. Instead he and Dog-of-the-Sea-Waves played together and got into all kinds of trouble. They terrorized the fish Nāʻale was trying to catch. They made a mess of the beach where Hōkū was drying food. They played with Makani's ropes and accidentally pulled ʻŌpua's gourds off the boat, tripping Makani, who fell into the water.

No one laughed. The two were separated, and Manu was put to work.

Manu gathered berries for Hōkū. He caught fish for Nāʻale. He fetched water for ʻŌpua. He twisted rope for Makani. But every evening after his work was done, he slipped off to meet his friend, and they played in the waves until it got too dark to see. Then Manu swam ashore, and Dog-of-the-Sea-Waves went hunting for food.

After many months of hard work, the boat was finally ready to leave. At the last moment, Manu dived into the water to say goodbye to Dog-of-the-Sea-Waves. As the brothers yelled for Manu to get aboard, Dog-of-the-Sea-Waves brushed his whiskers against Manu's cheek, then disappeared beneath the waves.

Hawaiian Raspberry

The brothers sailed down the island chain. When they came to the last island, 'Ōpua said, "Is that a cloud on the side of that mountain, or smoke? Let's go see."

Curious, the brothers anchored their boat in a quiet bay and swam ashore.

Halfway up the mountain, Makani felt a warm wind and hesitated. But his brothers told him not to worry.

After a few more steps, Manu noticed that the birds were silent. But his brothers paid no attention.

Then—a jolt!

The earth heaved up and slammed the brothers to the ground. Deep cracks appeared, then flames.

Hōkū grabbed Manu's hand, and the brothers fled down the slope. But a river of fire cut them off from the sea and forced them to the cliffs.

The earth shuddered, and the five brothers jumped—into the sea far below.

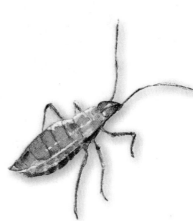

Wekiu Bug

ANALYZE THE TEXT

Analyze Illustrations How does the illustration help you feel what is described in the text?

But the sea they landed in was a monster. It thrashed from the earthquakes. It hissed from the burning lava. It lashed out at the brothers and grabbed Manu. In an instant, he was gone.

Makani filled his lungs with air and went to the very depths of the ocean, but there was no sign of Manu. ʻŌpua, with his voice like thunder, shouted for Manu above the crashing waves, but there was no answer. Nāʻale, who loved the sea, begged it to be calm, but it wouldn't listen.

Dragon Moray

All this time, Manu was fighting to get to the surface, but the sea wouldn't let go. Then he felt the whiskers. Manu clasped his arms around Dog-of-the-Sea-Waves, and up they went.

Pompom Crab

It was Hōkū who spotted them. The brothers raced toward Manu and cradled him above the waves.

"Manu, Manu," they cried over and over as they made their way to the boat. And to Dog-of-the-Sea-Waves they chanted their thanks:

Dog-that-swims-the-depths,
Dog-that-braves-the-currents,
Dog-that-knows-the-sea,
Dog-that-cares-for-our-brother.

The brothers then weighed anchor and headed for the southern sea and home. Manu stood on the deck and listened to Dog-of-the-Sea-Waves barking goodbye.

"We'll be back," Manu shouted.

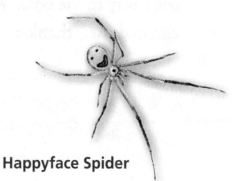

Happyface Spider

And when they returned, they came with their families. They embraced the land and made it their home.

ANALYZE THE TEXT

Author's Purpose Tell in your own words what you think the author wants readers to learn from the brothers' story.

Dig Deeper

How to Analyze the Text

Use these pages to learn about Author's Purpose and Analyzing Illustrations. Then read *Dog-of-the-Sea-Waves* again to apply what you learned.

Author's Purpose

Authors write for different reasons. The **author's purpose** may be to inform, to persuade readers to do or believe something, to describe, or to entertain. Sometimes an author has more than one purpose.

To help identify the author's purpose, think about text evidence in the story. Why were certain details included?

Look back at page 316 in *Dog-of-the-Sea-Waves*. On this page the author sets the scene and introduces you to the characters. You can already tell that it is a story of long ago. As you read, think about how other details point to the author's reason for writing.

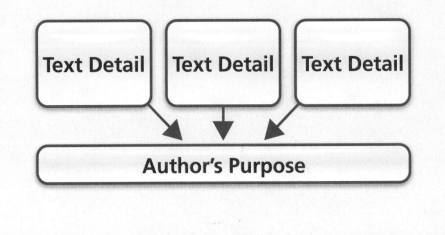

| Text Detail | Text Detail | Text Detail |

Author's Purpose

RL.3.1 ask and answer questions to demonstrate understanding, referring to the text; **RL.3.7** explain how illustrations contribute to the words

Analyze Illustrations

Illustrations like the paintings in *Dog-of-the-Sea-Waves* show the events of a story. They can also create a **mood**, or feeling, for the story. For example, in the illustration on page 324, the brothers look frightened. The dark blue waves are high and dangerous. Manu is being carried away by the sea. The mood is tense and scary.

Your Turn

Turn and Talk Review the story with a partner to prepare to discuss this question: *What changes do volcanoes cause?* Take turns speaking and listening carefully. Support your ideas with text evidence from the story.

Classroom Conversation

Continue your discussion of *Dog-of-the-Sea-Waves* by explaining your answers to these questions:

1 In what ways is Manu like his brothers? In what ways is he different?

2 What do the brothers learn from Dog-of-the-Sea-Waves?

3 What are some things you learned about Hawaii from this story?

Response Describe how the brothers feel about Dog-of-the-Sea-Waves when they first find him near the beginning of the story. How do they feel toward him in the middle of the story? How do their feelings change by the end? Write a paragraph that answers these questions. Use text evidence to support your answers.

Writing Tip

Organize the ideas in your paragraph in sequence. Use linking words and phrases such as *at first*, *then*, *later*, and *in the end* to show how the ideas are related.

COMMON CORE **RL.3.1** ask and answer questions to demonstrate understanding, referring to the text; **W.3.2a** introduce a topic and group related information/ include illustrations; **W.3.2b** develop the topic with facts, defintions, and details; **W.3.2c** use linking words and phrases to connect ideas within categories of information; **W.3.10** write routinely over extended time frames or short time frames; **SL.3.1a** come to discussions prepared/ explicitly draw on preparation and other information about the topic; **SL.3.1d** explain own ideas and understanding in light of the discussion

INFORMATIONAL TEXT

The Land Volcanoes Built

COMMON CORE **RI.3.7** use information gained from illustrations and words to demonstrate understanding; **RI.3.10** read and comprehend informational texts

The Land Volcanoes Built

by Patricia Ann Lynch

The islands of Hawaii spread over many miles of ocean. Eight large islands and 124 small ones are in the chain.

Each island is really the top of a mountain that pokes out of the sea. How were these islands formed? The answer is *volcanoes*.

What Is a Volcano?

A volcano is an opening, or vent, that goes deep into Earth. Deep within Earth it is so hot that rock melts. The melted rock is called magma.

Sometimes magma is pushed up and pours out of the volcano. Then the magma is called lava. The lava cools and hardens. It builds up. Over time, it can form a tall mountain. Each of the Hawaiian Islands formed in this way.

A Volcano Erupts

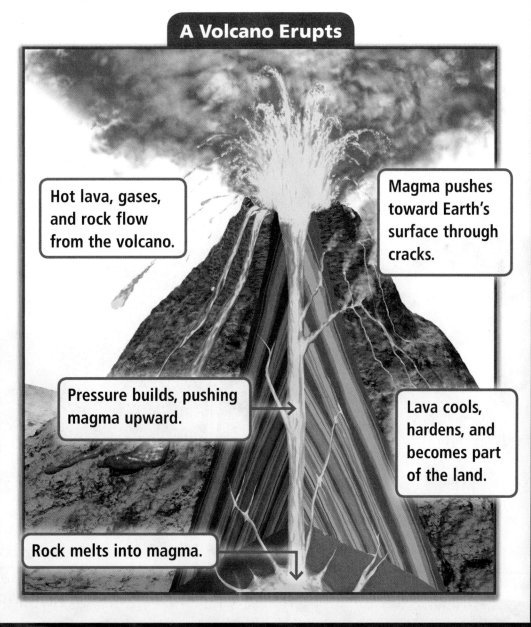

Hot lava, gases, and rock flow from the volcano.

Magma pushes toward Earth's surface through cracks.

Pressure builds, pushing magma upward.

Lava cools, hardens, and becomes part of the land.

Rock melts into magma.

Life Arrives

At first, the islands were bare. Waves rippled on empty shores. Life came much later. Wind and water carried plant seeds. Sea animals such as monk seals swam there. Other animals made the voyage aboard objects floating in the sea. The arrival of birds brought song.

The first people paddled in canoes from other islands. The stars guided them across the Pacific Ocean. The travelers spotted the islands. They dropped anchor in a calm bay and came ashore. The new islands were good places to live. There was plenty of fresh water to drink and lots of food. The leaves of the coconut tree could be used to build thatched shelters. Coconut husks could be twisted into strong ropes. These people became the first Hawaiians.

People from China, Japan, Samoa, the Philippines, and other countries live in Hawaii today.

Compare Texts

Compare Descriptions Think about the way the volcano erupted in *Dog-of-the-Sea-Waves*. With a partner, compare and contrast that description with what you learned about volcanoes in *The Land Volcanoes Built*. Use evidence from both texts to explain your ideas.

Write About It Imagine you are one of the brothers in *Dog-of-the-Sea-Waves*. Write to describe what you might see when you arrive at one of the islands. Use the information from *Dog-of-the-Sea-Waves* and *The Land Volcanoes Built* to guide you.

Analyze Relationships Review *Aero and Officer Mike* from Lesson 14 with a partner. Think about the relationship Officer Mike has with Aero. How is their real-life relationship similar to Manu's relationship with Dog-of-the-Sea-Waves? How is it different? Discuss your answers with your partner.

COMMON CORE **RL.3.1** ask and answer questions to demonstrate understanding, referring to the text; **RI.3.1** ask and answer questions to demonstrate understanding, referring to the text; **RI.3.9** compare and contrast important points and details in texts on the same topic; **W.3.10** write routinely over extended time frames or short time frames

Grammar

Complex Sentences A **complex sentence** has two parts. The main part could stand alone as a simple sentence. The other part is called a **dependent clause.** It could not stand alone as a sentence because it does not express a complete thought. A dependent clause is joined to the main part with a connecting word called a **subordinating conjunction**. Some subordinating conjunctions are *because, after, when,* and *if.*

Main Part	Dependent Clause
A volcano is dangerous	because its lava is hot.
The lava becomes rock	after it cools.
I saw a volcano	when I visited Hawaii.
You should visit Hawaii	if you can.

Try This! Copy each sentence. Then underline the main part of the sentence once. Underline the dependent clause twice.

1. An island forms when a mountain pokes out of the sea.

2. We flew to Hawaii because my grandma lives there.

Write a complex sentence for each pair of simple sentences. Use the subordinating conjunction in parentheses.

3. We will hike around the volcano. (if) We have time.

4. My grandma moved to Hawaii. (after) I was born.

Many short simple sentences in a row can sound choppy. You can make your writing more interesting if you include a few complex sentences. Here are more subordinating conjunctions you can use:

although	before	though	until
as	since	unless	while

You can also start a sentence with a dependent clause. Follow it with a comma.

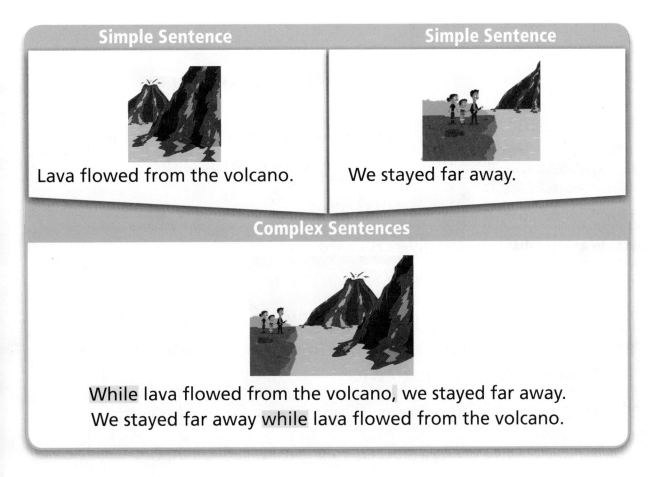

Simple Sentence

Lava flowed from the volcano.

Simple Sentence

We stayed far away.

Complex Sentences

While lava flowed from the volcano, we stayed far away.
We stayed far away while lava flowed from the volcano.

 **Connect Grammar to Writing**

As you revise your narrative next week, include some complex sentences. If two simple sentences sound choppy, join them with a subordinating conjunction.

W.3.3a establish a situation and introduce a narrator or characters/organize an event sequence; **W.3.3b** use dialogue and descriptions to develop experiences and events or show characters' responses; **W.3.3d** provide a sense of closure; **W.3.5** develop and strengthen writing by planning, revising, and editing

Narrative Writing

Reading–Writing Workshop: Prewrite

✓**Ideas** Once you have chosen a topic for a story, or **fictional narrative**, explore your topic. Think about it and fill a page with ideas.

Louis decided to write a story about pioneers. He began by listing details about his characters, setting, and plot. Then he made a story map and added even more details.

Writing Process Checklist

▶ **Prewrite**

☑ Did I pick a topic that my audience and I will enjoy?

☑ Did I decide what my characters and setting are like?

☑ Did I plan a good beginning, middle, and ending?

☑ Did I think of enough details?

Draft

Revise

Edit

Publish and Share

Exploring a Topic

Who? a family in a covered wagon
mother, father, son

Where and when? a desert

about 1850

What? get stuck in a sandstorm
uncomfortable and afraid

Setting

The desert in 1850, during a sandstorm inside a covered wagon, hot, crowded with furniture

Characters

Sam: scared, tired of waiting

Ma: hopeful

Pop: calm, cheerful, good storyteller

Plot

Beginning   Sam and his family have been stuck in a sandstorm for ten hours.

Middle   Sam is hot and scared. Pop tells him not to worry. Ma talks about their new home out West.

Ending   Pop tells Sam a story. Pop's story helps Sam relax until the storm ends.

Reading as a Writer

Which of Louis's details help you picture what is happening? What details can you add to your own story map to make the plot clear?

When I organized my fictional narrative, I added more details.

approached
section
avalanches
increases
equipment
tanks
slopes
altitude
succeed
halt

Vocabulary Reader   Context Cards

L.3.6 acquire and use conversational, general academic, and domain-specific words and phrases

Vocabulary in Context

1 approached

Climbers approached this mountain from the west. Slowly, they got nearer to it.

2 section

The top section, or part, of this mountain is the steepest.

3 avalanches

When avalanches occur, the powerful sliding snow can knock trees down.

4 increases

When storms blow in, the danger to climbers increases, or becomes greater.

Go Digital

▶ Study each Context Card.

▶ Ask a question that uses one of the Vocabulary words.

---

5 equipment

Mountain climbers check their supplies, or equipment, before a climb.

---

6 tanks

Tanks that hold oxygen help climbers breathe in the high, thin air.

---

7 slopes

Gentle slopes near the bottom of the mountain are easiest to climb.

---

8 altitude

The altitude, or height, of Granite Peak in Montana is 12,799 feet.

---

9 succeed

Everyone's goal is to reach the summit. If climbers plan well, they will succeed!

---

10 halt

Climbers come to a halt when it gets dark. They stop for the night.

Read and Comprehend

Go Digital

☑ TARGET SKILL

Text and Graphic Features As you read *Mountains: Surviving on Mt. Everest*, note how the author uses **text features** and **graphic features** such as headings, maps, diagrams, and charts to explain and make the information clear. Use a chart like this one to list the text and graphic features in the selection. Think about why the author uses them and how they add to the information in the text.

Text or Graphic Feature	Page	Purpose

☑ TARGET STRATEGY

Infer/Predict Use the text and graphic features to help you **predict** what you will learn and to **infer**, or figure out, what the author considers most important about the topic.

COMMON CORE

RI.3.5 use text features and search tools to locate information; **RI.3.7** use information gained from illustrations and words to demonstrate understanding

344

Mountains

Mountains are high, elevated landforms that are found all over the world. Some are high and snow-capped. Others are rounded and covered with trees. Still others are smoking volcanoes. The most common kind are fold mountains, such as the Alps in Europe. These were created long ago when two plates of Earth's crust collided.

In *Mountains: Surviving on Mt. Everest,* you'll read about a 16-year-old boy who climbs Mount Everest, the tallest mountain on Earth.

ANCHOR TEXT

TARGET SKILL

Text and Graphic Features

Tell how text and graphic features help you find information.

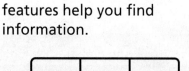
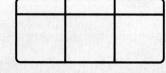

GENRE

Informational text gives you facts about a topic. As you read, look for:

▶ headings that tell about the content of sections
▶ photographs and captions
▶ graphic features such as maps and diagrams

COMMON CORE **RI.3.2** determine the main idea/recount details and explain how they support the main idea; **RI.3.5** use text features and search tools to locate information; **RI.3.7** use information gained from illustrations and words to demonstrate understanding

MEET THE AUTHOR

Michael Sandler

Michael Sandler enjoys extreme adventures. He loves to travel and has been to the foothills of Mount Everest, the highest mountain in the world. Several years ago while touring Africa, he got lost in the Sahara, the world's largest desert. That adventure might have helped him later to write *Deserts: Surviving in the Sahara*.

Other extreme books by Sandler include *Oceans: Surviving in the Deep Sea* and *Rain Forests: Surviving in the Amazon*.

Mountains

Surviving on Mt. Everest

by Michael Sandler

ESSENTIAL QUESTION

Why do mountain climbers need to be well prepared?

Climbing Mount Everest

The clock showed almost midnight. The temperature was freezing. Icy winds roared by.

A group of people huddled in the darkness on a rocky ridge. In moments, they would begin the final stage of a dangerous journey. They were climbing to the top of Mount Everest, the world's highest mountain.

Among the climbers was Temba Tsheri (SHUHR ee) Sherpa. Just two weeks before, Temba had celebrated his 16th birthday. Now he was trying to survive in one of the world's most extreme places. Making it to the top of Everest was Temba's dream. He would be the youngest person ever to reach the summit, which is 29,035 feet (8,850 meters) high.

What Are Mountains?

Mountains are a type of tall landform. They rise high above the area around them. Mountains are taller than hills. They can rise thousands of feet (kilometers) in the air. They are found all over the world, even beneath the sea.

A group of mountains is called a range. The biggest mountain range in North America is the Rocky Mountains. The Andes (AN deez), in South America, is the world's longest mountain range.

Mount Everest, the mountain Temba was climbing, is part of the Himalaya (hihm uh LAY uh) Mountains. The name "Himalaya" means "home of snow." This Asian range is the world's highest. It includes nine of the ten tallest mountains on Earth.

Mountains cover one quarter of Earth's land surface.

Mountain Conditions

As Temba approached Everest's summit, survival became harder and harder. Mountain conditions get more extreme the higher a person climbs.

Air contains less and less oxygen as the altitude increases. Breathing becomes nearly impossible. Thin air can cause headaches and dizziness at 10,000 feet (3,048 meters). Higher up, it can be deadly.

Humans cannot survive for long at the top section of mountains like Everest. Hurricane-force winds can reach 130 miles per hour (209 kph). Temperatures can plummet to –100F (–73C) during the night. Blowing snow makes it hard to see. Temba was headed here.

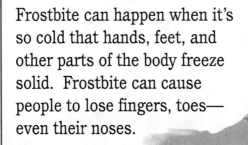

Frostbite can happen when it's so cold that hands, feet, and other parts of the body freeze solid. Frostbite can cause people to lose fingers, toes— even their noses.

Why Do People Climb Mountains?

People climb mountains for many reasons. Some enjoy the thrill of being high above the clouds. Others like the challenge of testing their skills.

For decades, however, reaching the top of Everest was a test that no climber could pass. The first attempts to climb Everest were made during the 1920s. Again and again, the climbing teams stopped short of their goal. Avalanches, storms, sickness, and exhaustion brought them to a halt.

Then, in 1953, two climbers finally succeeded— Sir Edmund Hillary and Tenzing Norgay. Hillary was from New Zealand. Norgay was a Sherpa from Nepal (nuh PAWL).

ANALYZE THE TEXT

Text and Graphic Features These pages include headings, a caption, and a boxed fact. What kinds of information do these text features provide?

Sir Edmund Hillary (left) and Tenzing Norgay (right) show off their survival equipment in 1953.

Temba's Mistake

Temba had tried to climb Everest before. It ended, however, in failure.

"I didn't have enough training or proper equipment," Temba said. He was almost at the summit when his oxygen supply ran out.

Without oxygen, Temba couldn't think clearly. He made a terrible mistake. He took off his gloves to tie his boots. His fingers froze. Temba suffered frostbite on both hands. He had to turn back just 70 feet (21 meters) from his goal.

The next time around, however, Temba was prepared. He had trained hard. He had the right equipment, thanks to his classmates and teachers. They had raised money for his trip.

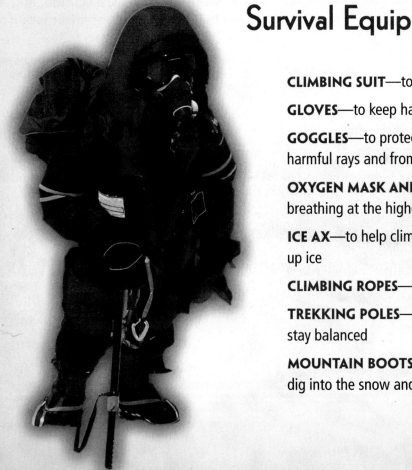

Survival Equipment

CLIMBING SUIT—to protect against cold

GLOVES—to keep hands warm and dry

GOGGLES—to protect eyes from the sun's harmful rays and from reflection off snow

OXYGEN MASK AND TANK—for breathing at the highest altitudes

ICE AX—to help climb slopes and break up ice

CLIMBING ROPES—to climb up slopes

TREKKING POLES—to help a climber stay balanced

MOUNTAIN BOOTS—with spikes that dig into the snow and ice

Camp-to-Camp

Temba's second try began in April 2001. Mount Everest sits between Nepal and Tibet (tuh BEHT). There are several different routes to the top. Temba would take a route from the north, the Tibetan side.

Climbers move from one camp to the next higher one and then rest for a while. At each camp, their bodies get used to the higher altitudes. Temba spent several weeks moving between camps with his team.

At Camp 3, the team waited for a break in the weather. Winter was over, but there had been a series of severe snowstorms. Getting caught in a snowstorm farther up the mountain would be deadly.

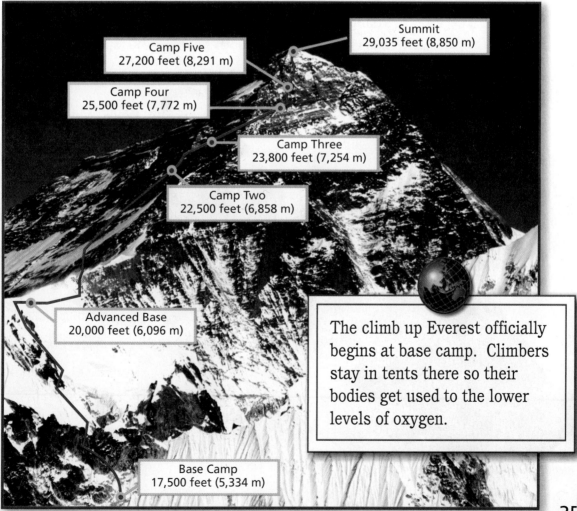

Summit
29,035 feet (8,850 m)

Camp Five
27,200 feet (8,291 m)

Camp Four
25,500 feet (7,772 m)

Camp Three
23,800 feet (7,254 m)

Camp Two
22,500 feet (6,858 m)

Advanced Base
20,000 feet (6,096 m)

The climb up Everest officially begins at base camp. Climbers stay in tents there so their bodies get used to the lower levels of oxygen.

Base Camp
17,500 feet (5,334 m)

The Climb Along the Ridge

On May 20, Temba's team reached Camp 4. Then the climbers headed out on the great ridge leading to the summit. Temba plunged his ax into ice walls, pulling himself up. He steadied himself against 50-mile-per-hour (80-kph) winds. Yet, he climbed higher and higher.

Temba had to move fast or die. Darkness stopped him before he got to Camp 5. His team had gone ahead. Luckily, Temba found a tent. He spent the night frightened and alone.

The next day, Temba rejoined his team. They reached Camp 6, one day's climb from their goal.

ANALYZE THE TEXT

Main Ideas and Details Which details in the text support the idea that climbing Mount Everest is dangerous and difficult?

Climbers have to be very careful. Towers of ice can fall over without warning.

Climbers use aluminum ladders to cross deep cracks in the ice, called crevasses. The crevasses are constantly opening and closing, so it is very dangerous.

Reaching the Top of the World

Just before midnight, Temba began his final climb. A headlamp lit the darkness. An oxygen mask helped Temba to breathe. Sometimes he'd stop to rest or to change oxygen bottles.

Just after sunrise, Temba reached Mount Everest's summit. He was higher than anyone else on the planet. Temba planted two flags. One was for his school. The other was for Nepal. "I felt so happy," he said.

It is dangerous for climbers to spend more than ten minutes at the top of Everest. The body needs to get to a lower altitude where there is more oxygen.

Temba was the youngest person to climb Mt. Everest.

Will the Mountains Survive?

Temba survived in the mountains. Now, he wants to make sure the mountains survive. The world's mountains face many different threats.

Trash is one problem. For a while, Everest was called the "world's highest garbage dump." The mountain was littered with tons of trash that climbers left behind—batteries, bottles, and empty oxygen tanks. Many climbers didn't have the time or strength to carry these things back down with them.

Climbers have left garbage on Everest since 1921. Now, people are trying to clean up the mess.

Global warming is another problem. As Earth gets warmer, mountain glaciers are melting. Himalayan lakes are swelling up with water. When they flood, mountain landscapes will be changed forever.

In 2005, the snowcap on Tanzania's Mount Kilimanjaro melted for the first time in history.

After the Climb

When Temba came down from Everest, he was thinking about food, not fame. After weeks of camping, he was starving for home cooking.

Still, when he flew home to Kathmandu, a huge crowd was waiting. Temba couldn't believe it. "I had never seen so many cameras. . . . All of them were pointed at me," he said.

Despite the attention, Temba focused on his schoolwork. He needed a good education to achieve his other dream, starting a school in Dolakha.

Will Temba succeed? Only time will tell. If you've survived on Everest, however, and reached the top, no goal seems too high!

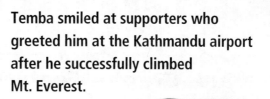

Temba smiled at supporters who greeted him at the Kathmandu airport after he successfully climbed Mt. Everest.

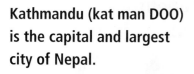

Kathmandu (kat man DOO) is the capital and largest city of Nepal.

Dig Deeper

How to Analyze the Text

Use these pages to learn about Text and Graphic Features and Main Ideas and Details. Then read *Mountains: Surviving on Mt. Everest* again to apply what you learned.

Text and Graphic Features

Informational text like *Mountains: Surviving on Mt. Everest* may use different kinds of text and graphic features to present information.

Text features include headings that tell about the content of sections. Captions identify what is in photographs. Boxed facts can add to information found in the main text.

Graphic features may include a map to help locate a place. A labeled diagram will show the parts of something. Photos and illustrations show what things look like.

Look back at pages 348 through 351. How can you find out more about mountains?

Text or Graphic Feature	Page	Purpose

RI.3.2 determine the main idea/recount details and explain how they support the main idea; **RI.3.5** use text features and search tools to locate information; **RI.3.7** use information gained from illustrations and words to demonstrate understanding

Main Ideas and Details

An author may write each part of an informational text around an important idea, or **main idea**. Facts, or **details**, are included to tell more about, or support, the main idea.

In the first section of *Mountains: Surviving on Mt. Everest*, the author tells about Temba Tsheri Sherpa. The main idea is that Temba is about to become the youngest person ever to reach the summit of Mount Everest. Look for details that tell more about this.

Your Turn

RETURN TO THE ESSENTIAL QUESTION

 Review the selection with a partner to prepare to discuss this question: *Why do mountain climbers need to be well prepared?* Use text features to find evidence in the text that supports your ideas.

Classroom Conversation

Continue your discussion of *Mountains: Surviving Mt. Everest* by explaining your answers to these questions:

1. What does Temba learn from experience about the right way to climb Mount Everest?

2. Why do you think Temba is surprised by the crowd that greeted him in Kathmandu?

3. Would you want to climb a mountain? Why or why not?

Response Think about why Temba wanted to reach the top of Mount Everest. Write a paragraph to describe and explain his dream. Use text evidence from the selection to support your opinions.

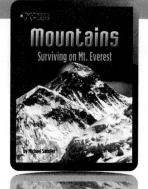

Writing Tip

When describing Temba's dream and Mount Everest, choose strong adjectives and adverbs to create a vivid picture.

COMMON CORE **RI.3.1** ask and answer questions to demonstrate understanding, referring to the text; **RI.3.5** use text features and search tools to locate information; **W.3.1a** introduce the topic, state an opinion, and create an organizational structure; **SL.3.1a** come to discussions prepared/explicitly draw on preparation and other information about the topic; **SL.3.1d** explain own ideas and understanding in light of the discussion; **L.3.3a** choose words and phrases for effect

PLAY

The BIG Cleanup

by Kate McGovern

Cast of Characters

Scott, leader of the "Clean Trails" team

Talia, a team member

Ricky, a team member

(*A special team is preparing to clear garbage from Sunshine Point Park.*)

Scott: Many people love to hike and camp in these hills. Some of them leave trash behind. We're going to help clean up! Does everyone have his or her equipment?

Talia: (*holding up her trash bags*) I do. These bags are for carrying down trash.

Ricky: These hiking boots will make it easier for us to climb the hills.

(*They arrive at a messy campsite.*)

Scott: (*looking around and frowning*) Many hikers stopped here to rest as they approached the next hill. They left bottles, food containers, and even a tent!

Ricky: People shouldn't treat the outdoors like a garbage dump! Nature is for everyone to enjoy.

Talia: Let's pick up this mess! When spring comes and the snow melts, we don't want trash to wash into the river.

Scott: (*waving them onward*) Let's go! This is the last section to climb.

Talia: This section is a lot trickier to climb in the winter. I'm glad the park ranger thought of adding this rope!

Scott: When we get to the top, we'll stop to rest. It's a clear day, so we should be able to see town from up there.

Ricky: I can't wait for a break. Let us remember to take our snack wrappers back down with us.

Scott: Yes! If we all do our part, Sunshine Point can stay clean for a long time.

Compare Texts

TEXT TO TEXT

Compare Activities Compare and contrast Temba's adventure on Mount Everest with what the characters do in *The Big Cleanup*. Use text evidence, photos, and illustrations to support your discussion. What kind of climbing equipment do they use? What do they want to do to help the mountain?

TEXT TO SELF

Climbing a Mountain Would you like to climb Mount Everest like Temba in *Mountains: Surviving on Mt. Everest*? Why or why not? Take turns telling a partner. Listen to each other and ask questions.

TEXT TO WORLD

Work in Extreme Places Reread *Life on the Ice* from Lesson 20. Think about what it's like being a scientist in Antarctica. How is that like being a mountain climber on Mt. Everest? How is it different? Share your ideas with a partner. Use evidence from the texts to support your answers.

Go Digital

COMMON CORE **RL.3.7** explain how illustrations contribute to the words; **RI.3.1** ask and answer questions to demonstrate understanding, referring to the text; **RI.3.7** use information gained from illustrations and words to demonstrate understanding; **RI.3.9** compare and contrast important points and details in texts on the same topic

Grammar

More, Most, -er, -est You can use **adjectives** and **adverbs** to describe and to make comparisons.

- Adjectives describe nouns. Adverbs describe verbs.

- Use adjectives or adverbs that end in *-er* to compare two. Use adjectives or adverbs that end in *-est* to compare more than two.

- When an adjective or adverb has three or more syllables, use *more* to compare two and *most* to compare more than two. Also use *more* and *most* with adverbs ending in *-ly*.

	Compare Two	**Compare More Than Two**
Adjective	*This trail is* steeper *than that one.*	*This trail is the* safest *of all the trails.*
Adverb	*She walked* more carefully *than I did.*	*These boots feel* most comfortable *of all.*

 **Write each sentence with the correct form of the adjective or adverb in parentheses.**

1. This is the _____ story I have read. (more exciting, most exciting)

2. Temba tried _____ of all the climbers. (harder, hardest)

3. The wind howls _____ at night than in the day. (louder, loudest)

4. The mountain top is _____ than the bottom. (colder, coldest)

You can help readers picture your ideas when you use adjectives and adverbs. These describe what things look like or how actions happen. If you want to make comparisons, think about what is compared and how many. Then choose an adjective or an adverb with the correct ending, or use *more* or *most*.

Choose the warmest gloves you can find.

Try on a larger size boot than the size you usually wear.

You will climb the next mountain more easily with strong ropes.

 **Connect Grammar to Writing**

As you write your narrative, look for places where you can use adjectives and adverbs to describe and to compare. Choose the correct form to compare two or more than two things or actions.

W.3.3a establish a situation and introduce a narrator or characters/organize an event sequence; **W.3.3b** use dialogue and descriptions to develop experiences and events or show characters' responses; **W.3.3c** use temporal words and phrases to signal event order; **W.3.3d** provide a sense of closure; **W.3.5** develop and strengthen writing by planning, revising, and editing

Narrative Writing

Reading–Writing Workshop: Revise

✔ **Word Choice** Good writers try to make you feel what their characters are feeling. They use strong words to put you in the middle of the events. When you revise your **fictional narrative**, use words that will make your writing exciting.

Louis drafted his story about a family stuck in a sandstorm. When he revised, he added some stronger words and time-order words.

Revised Draft

> The sandstorm had been going on for
> ~~a long time.~~ ^ten hours^ Sam and his parents ^hid^ ~~were~~
>
> inside their covered wagon. The wind
> blew faster ^and louder^ than Sam ever remembered.
>
> ~~It blew louder too.~~ The sand was ^whipping^ ~~moving~~
>
> around them.
>
> Sam and his family were moving out
>
> West.

Writing Process Checklist

Prewrite

Draft

▶ **Revise**

- ✔ Did I introduce the characters, setting, and problem in an interesting way?

- ✔ Does the middle part show how the characters deal with the problem?

- ✔ Does the ending show how the problem works out?

- ✔ Did I use time-order words to show when events happened?

Edit

Publish and Share

Sandstorm!

by Louis Hudson

The sandstorm had been going on for ten hours. Sam and his parents hid inside their covered wagon. The wind blew faster and louder than Sam ever remembered. The sand was whipping around them.

Sam and his family were moving out West. They had been on the trail for two weeks already. Their wagon was full of everything they owned. There was barely enough room to sit. Hot and sweaty, Sam asked, "How long will we have to wait?" His voice was shaky.

Pop told Sam not to worry. The storm would soon end. Ma talked about what their new life would be like. She had lived in the crowded, dusty city for thirty years. Now she dreamed of living in open fields.

Then Pop began to tell stories of his childhood. He had three brothers, and there were many adventures to tell! Sam enjoyed the stories so much that when the storm died down two hours later, he hardly even noticed.

Test POWER

Read "The Big Day" and "Starring Maria." As you read, stop and answer each question using text evidence.

The Big Day

It seemed to Maria that her whole family was making a ridiculous fuss over her sister Lucy's fifteenth birthday. Maria's parents were born in Mexico, where it was a tradition to have a big party for a girl turning fifteen. The celebration was called a Quinceañera (KEEN say an YAY ra).

At first, Maria had been as excited about the party as Lucy was. There would be a real live band playing in a tent in their backyard. Their grandparents were coming from Mexico. Lucy kept saying everything was going to be wonderful, but by now Maria was beginning to think it would be wonderful when the party was over.

Planning the party was so much work! Maria had been in charge of collecting all the addresses for the invitations and typing them on the computer. She had printed out address labels for all the envelopes. She had helped create the fancy decorations. She had spent many hours on these tasks, but everyone else was so busy getting ready for Lucy's party that Maria felt as if no one noticed her at all.

> **1** What tasks has Maria spent hours on? Include examples from the story in your response.

The night before the party, Maria was in her room when Lucy knocked on her door. "I have something to show you," Lucy said. "I bought it with my babysitting money."

RL.3.1 ask and answer questions to demonstrate understanding, referring to the text; **RL.3.3** describe characters and explain how their actions contribute to the sequence of events; **RL.3.5** refer to parts of stories, dramas, and poems/describe how each part builds on earlier sections; **RL3.9** compare and contrast themes, settings, and plots of stories by the same author

Lucy handed Maria a small box. Maria opened it and lifted out a necklace that sparkled in the light. Maria guessed that Lucy had bought it to wear for her party. "Oh, Lucy, it's beautiful!" she exclaimed.

"I'm glad you like it," said Lucy, "because I got it for you! You have worked so hard to get everything ready for my party. This is my way of saying thank you."

---

2 What does the ending show about the kind of person Lucy is? Use details from the story to support your response.

Starring Maria

Chapter One
The Good News

Maria couldn't wait to share the good news with her parents and her sister Lucy. By the time they all sat down at the dinner table, she felt ready to burst with excitement. "You'll never guess what happened today!" she exclaimed. The rest of the family cheered when Maria announced that she had been given a leading role in her school play.

"It's a really big part, so I do have a lot of lines to learn," she explained, with a little less enthusiam.

"Don't worry about that, Maria," Lucy told her. "I'll help you learn your lines and rehearse them with you."

After dinner, the girls hurried to get their homework done so they could start rehearsing. Lucy helped Maria rehearse every day, and Maria got better and better.

Chapter Two
Maria's Big Night

The busy weeks had flown by, and now it was the night of the class play. Maria peeked out from backstage and saw that the auditorium was packed. She was happy to see that her parents and Lucy had found seats right up front.

As she stepped out onto the stage, Maria felt a bit anxious. Suppose she made a mistake in front of all those people! As soon as she spoke her first line, though, she began to feel better. All that rehearsing she had done with Lucy had really helped.

> **3** How did events you read about in Chapter One affect events in Chapter Two?

Then, halfway through the play, disaster struck. Maria's character was supposed to be cheering up one of the other characters. But Maria couldn't remember her next line! She looked around wildly and noticed Lucy leaning forward, moving her mouth silently. Maria watched her carefully. "You're doing a great job!" Lucy was saying.

At first, Maria thought Lucy was just trying to encourage her, but then she realized what Lucy was really doing. Maria turned to the other character and said her next line, "You're doing a great job!" The play went on, and Maria knew that she was doing a great job, too.

> **4** How are the themes and plots of these two stories by the same author alike, and how are they different?

This glossary contains meanings and pronunciations for some of the words in this book. The Full Pronunciation Key shows how to pronounce each consonant and vowel in a special spelling. At the bottom of the glossary pages is a shortened form of the full key.

Full Pronunciation Key

Consonant Sounds

b	bib, cabbage	kw	choir, quick	t	tight, stopped
ch	church, stitch	l	lid, needle, tall	th	bath, thin
d	deed, mailed, puddle	m	am, man, dumb	th	bathe, this
f	fast, fife, off, phrase, rough	n	no, sudden	v	cave, valve, vine
g	gag, get, finger	ng	thing, ink	w	with, wolf
h	hat, who	p	pop, happy	y	yes, yolk, onion
hw	which, where	r	roar, rhyme	z	rose, size, xylophone, zebra
j	judge, gem	s	miss, sauce, scene, see	zh	garage, pleasure, vision
k	cat, kick, school	sh	dish, ship, sugar, tissue		

Vowel Sounds

ă	pat, laugh	ŏ	horrible, pot	ŭ	cut, flood, rough, some
ā	ape, aid, pay	ō	go, row, toe, though	û	circle, fur, heard, term, turn, urge, word
â	air, care, wear	ô	all, caught, for, paw		
ä	father, koala, yard	oi	boy, noise, oil	yōo	cure
ĕ	pet, pleasure, any	ou	cow, out	yōo	abuse, use
ē	be, bee, easy, piano	ŏŏ	full, book, wolf	ə	ago, silent, pencil, lemon, circus
ĭ	if, pit, busy	ōō	boot, rude, fruit, flew		
ī	ride, by, pie, high				
î	dear, deer, fierce, mere				

Stress Marks

Primary Stress ´: bi·ol·o·gy [bī ŏl´ ə jē]
Secondary Stress ´: bi·o·log·i·cal [bī´ ə lŏj´ ĭ kəl]

Pronunciation key and definitions copyright (c) 2007 by Houghton Mifflin Harcourt Publishing Company. Reproduced by permission from The American Heritage Children's Dictionary and The American Heritage Student Dictionary.

A

a·board (ə **bôrd´**) *adverb and preposition* On, onto, or inside a vehicle, such as a ship, train, or bus: *The captain welcomed us **aboard** as we stepped onto the ship's deck.*

ab·sorb (əb **sôrb´**) *verb* Take in or soak up: *A sponge can **absorb** lots of water.*

ac·ci·dent (**ăk´** sĭ dənt) *noun* An event that is not expected and not wanted: *Traffic was held up by two **accidents** on the highway.*

al·ti·tude (**ăl´** tĭ tōōd´) *noun* A height measured from sea level or from the earth's surface: *The plane flew at an **altitude** of 30,000 feet.*

an·chor (**ăng´** kər) *noun* A heavy metal object, attached to a ship, that is dropped overboard to keep the ship in place: *It took two sailors to raise the heavy **anchor** when the ship was ready to sail.*

ap·proach (ə **prōch´**) *verb* To come near or nearer: *As the storm **approached**, people were told to leave their seaside homes.*

ar·riv·al (ə **rī´** vəl) *noun* The act of reaching a place: *We waited for the **arrival** of our guests.*

av·a·lanche (**ăv´** ə lănch´) *noun* A large amount of snow, ice, or earth that falls down a mountain: *Skiers should be warned of the danger of **avalanches** on this mountain.*

B

base (bās) *noun* The lowest part; bottom: *We camped at the **base** of the cliff.*

bat (băt) *verb* To hit or tap: *The baby **batted** at the ball playfully, trying to make it roll.*

bay (bā) *noun* A part of the sea that cuts into the land: *Have you ever seen sharks swimming in this **bay**?*

bur·den (**bûr´** dən) *noun* A heavy or difficult load to be carried: *Donkeys are often used to carry a **burden**.*

bur·y (**běr´** ē) *verb* Cover from view; hide: *I **buried** my face in the pillow.*

buzz (bûz) *verb* To make a low, humming sound like a bee: *The mosquitoes are **buzzing**, and I can't get to sleep.*

ă rat / ā pay / â care / ä father / ě pet / ē be / ĭ pit / ī pie / î fierce / ŏ pot / ō go / ô paw, for / oi oil / ōō book

C

car·ton (**kär´** tn) *noun* A cardboard box used to hold goods: *Let's pack these gifts into a mailing* **carton.**

chill·y (**chĭl´** ē) *adjective* Unpleasantly cold: *Please take a jacket if the weather is damp and* **chilly.**

clat·ter (**klăt´** ûr) *verb* To make a rattling sound: *The pots and pans* **clattered** *as they fell on the floor.*

cli·mate (**klī´** mĭt) *noun* The usual weather that occurs in a place: *The* **climate** *in polar areas is very harsh.*

clue (klo͞o) *noun* Something that helps to solve a problem or mystery: *Here are some more* **clues** *to the riddle.*

clump (klŭmp) *noun* Thick cluster or group: *Watch out for* **clumps** *of poison ivy along the path!*

col·o·ny (**kŏl´** ə nē) *noun* A group of living things of the same kind living or growing together: *A* **colony** *of bees built a hive in the tree.*

com·pli·ca·ted (**kŏm´** plĭ kā´ tĭd) *adjective* Not easy to understand, deal with, or solve: *Did you do the* **complicated** *problem on page 5?*

con·sole (kən sōl´) *verb* To make someone feel less sad: *Rosa's friends tried to* **console** *her when she didn't make the soccer team.*

con·stant (**kŏn´** stənt) *adjective* Without a break or pause: *The car is in* **constant** *use.*

con·ver·sa·tion (**kŏn´** vər sā´ shən) *noun* Informal talk between two or more people: *My sister has some long phone* **conversations** *with her friends.*

cov·er·ing (**kŭv´** ər ĭng) *noun* Something that covers: *If it rains during our camping trip, we can put waterproof* **coverings** *on the tents.*

cur·rent·ly (**kûr´** ənt lē) *adverb* At the present time; now: *That movie is* **currently** *showing.*

D

dis·solve (dĭ **zŏlv´**) *verb* To change from a solid to a liquid: *To make hot chocolate,* **dissolve** *sugar and cocoa powder in hot milk.*

dra·mat·ic (drə **măt´** ĭk) *adjective* Exciting: *The* **dramatic** *ending of the play left the audience stunned.*

carton

clue

Clue is sometimes spelled *clew.* In a Greek myth, a prince named Theseus was jailed by King Minos. To escape, Theseus had to enter a maze, battle a creature called the Minotaur, and find his way out of the maze again. Theseus used a clew, a ball of thread, to guide him out of the maze.

---

o͞o b**oo**t / ou **ou**t / ŭ c**u**t / û f**u**r / hw **wh**ich / th **th**in / *th* **th**is / zh vi**si**on / ə **a**go, sil**e**nt, penc**i**l, lem**o**n, circ**u**s

drip (drĭp) *verb* To fall or let fall in drops: *Water is **dripping** into the attic from a leak in the roof.*

drow·sy (**drou** zē) *adjective* Sleepy: *The **drowsy** cat took a nap in the garden.*

drip

E

e·quip·ment (ĭ **kwĭp´** mənt) *noun* The things that are needed for a purpose: *This store sells camping **equipment.***

ev·i·dence (**ĕv´** ĭ dəns) *noun* Facts or signs that help one find out the truth or decide: *The broken window was **evidence** that a burglary had taken place.*

F

fetch (fĕch) *verb* To go and bring back: *Please **fetch** a book from the shelf so that I can read.*

fierce (fîrs) *adjective* Wild and savage; dangerous: *Tigers can be **fierce** animals.*

fos·sil (**fŏs´** əl) *noun* The remains or traces of a plant or animal of an earlier age: *These tiny **fossils** are the bones of ancient birds.*

fright·en·ing (**frīt´** nĭng) *adjective* Scary: *We spent a **frightening** few minutes listening to the bear outside our tent.*

G

glance (glănts) *verb* To look and quickly look away: *Just by **glancing** at the bear, I could tell that it was still quite young.*

glide (glīd) *verb* To move smoothly, quietly, and with ease: *Many skaters were **gliding** gracefully around the ice rink.*

glob·al (**glō´** bəl) *adjective* Worldwide; relating to the entire earth: *Many countries are cooperating in a **global** effort to end hunger.*

greed·i·ly (**grē´** də lē´) *adverb* In a way that shows you are taking or eating more than you need: *The little dog **greedily** ate all of its food and begged for more.*

guide (gīd) *verb* To show the way to; direct: *The ranger **guided** us along the park's trails.*

ă rat / ā p**a**y / â c**a**re / ä f**a**ther / ĕ p**e**t / ē b**e** / ĭ p**i**t / ī p**ie** / î f**ie**rce / ŏ p**o**t / ō g**o** / ô p**a**w, f**o**r / oi **o**il / o͝o b**oo**k

H

halt (hôlt) *verb* To come or bring to a stop: *Police will halt traffic to let the parade pass.*

hard·ly (härd´ lē) *adverb* Barely; only just: *This box is so heavy I can hardly lift it.*

he·ro·ic (hə rō´ ĭk) *adjective* Like a hero; brave: *It is heroic when firefighters save people from burning buildings.*

hesitation (hĕ´ zĭ tā´ shən) *noun* A pause before doing something: *After some hesitation, I decided to try the broccoli.*

I

ig·nore (ĭg nôr´) *verb* To purposely pay no attention to: *Edwin ignores his alarm clock on the weekend.*

in·crease (ĭn krēs´) *verb* To make or become greater or larger: *As your height increases, you usually gain weight, too.*

in·spire (ĭn spīr´) *verb* To move to action: *The promise of money inspired me to work extra hard.*

L

land·scape (lănd´ skāp´) *noun* A stretch of land that is viewed as scenery: *We watched the desert landscape from the car window.*

la·va (lä´ və) *noun* Melted rock that flows from a volcano: *Hot lava oozed down the side of the volcano.*

lay·er (lā´ ər) *noun* A single thickness, coating, or sheet of material covering a surface: *Sprinkle a layer of cheese on top of the tomato sauce.*

load (lōd) *verb* To put into a vehicle or structure for carrying: *The dock workers loaded grain onto the ship.*

lo·ca·tion (lō kā´ shən) *noun* A place where something is or can be found: *We finally found the location of the airport.*

love·ly (lŭv´ lē) *adjective* Beautiful; very pleasing: *Their garden is the loveliest one I have ever seen.*

lava
The word *lava* comes from an Italian word. The Italian word, in turn, came from the Latin word *labes*, meaning "fall."

ōō b**oo**t / ou **ou**t / ŭ c**u**t / û f**u**r / hw **wh**ich / th **th**in / *th* **th**is / zh vi**si**on / ə **a**go, sil**e**nt, penc**i**l, lem**o**n, circ**u**s

M

man·age (**măn´** ĭj) *verb* To succeed in doing something: *I managed to finish my work ahead of time.*

mi·grate (**mī´** grāt) *verb* To move regularly from one region or climate to another: *Many birds migrate to warmer places for the winter.*

O

o·ver·heat·ed (ō´ vər **hēt´** ĭd) *adjective* Too hot: *Pets can easily get overheated on hot summer days.*

P

pas·sage (**păs** ĭj) *noun* Narrow pathway or channel: *Busy ants dig a maze of passages in each anthill.*

pleas·ure (**plĕzh´** ər) *noun* A feeling of happiness or enjoyment; delight: *She smiled with pleasure when she saw the puppies.*

plen·ty (**plĕn´** tē) *noun* A full supply or amount: *Children need plenty of exercise.*

pol·len (**pŏl´** ən) *noun* Tiny grains that fertilize female plants to produce seeds: *Flower pollen makes new plants grow, but it also makes me sneeze all spring!*

pol·lu·tion (pə **lōō´** shən) *noun* The act of making dirty, impure, or harmful; the condition of being dirty, impure, or harmful: *Smog is a kind of air pollution.*

prai·rie (**prâr´** ē) *noun* A large, mostly flat grassland with few trees: *Wheat and other grains grow well on the flat lands of the prairie.*

proj·ect (**prŏj´** ĕkt´) *noun* A plan for doing something; scheme: *The town's voters approved the building project.*

prove (prōōv) *verb* To show to be true by backing up with facts: *Getting an A on the test will prove that you studied.*

R

re·cy·cle (rē **sī´** kəl) *verb* To treat materials that have been thrown away in order to use them again: *Many cities recycle glass, cans, and newspapers.*

ă **r**a**t** / ā **p**a**y** / â **c**a**re** / ä **f**a**ther** / ĕ p**et** / ē **be** / ĭ **p**i**t** / ī **pie** / î **fie**r**ce** / ŏ p**ot** / ō g**o** / ô p**aw**, f**o**r / oi **oil** / ōō b**oo**k

re•gion (rē´ jən) *noun* A usually large area of the earth's surface: *This **region** receives very little rainfall each year.*

re•mains (rĭ **mānz´**) *noun* All or part of a dead body: *The **remains** of this polar bear were covered by ice for hundreds of years.*

re•un•ion (rē **yoōn´** yən) *noun* A gathering of the members of a group who have been separated: *Our family has a yearly **reunion**.*

rip•ple (rĭp´ əl) *verb* To form or cause to form small waves: *The surface of the river **rippled** when I skipped a stone across it.*

rough (rŭf) *adjective* Not smooth to the touch: *The outside of a pineapple is **rough**, but the skin of a banana is smooth.*

rub•bish (rŭb´ ĭsh) *noun* Trash: *Please take this **rubbish** out to the trash can.*

rus•tle (rŭs´ əl) *noun* A soft crackling sound like dry leaves: *I love to hear the **rustle** of paper when I unwrap a package.*

S

scold (skôld) *verb* To angrily tell someone about his or her mistakes: *Jake's mother was **scolding** him for being careless with his new toy.*

sec•tion (sĕk´ shən) *noun* A part taken from a whole: *A slice is a **section** of a cake or pie.*

shade (shād) *noun* An area that is partly dark because light has been blocked off from it: *It is too cold to sit in the **shade**.*

shel•ter (shĕl´ tər) *noun* Something that protects or covers: *Stand under the **shelter** at the bus stop if it's raining.*

sin•cere (sĭn **sîr´**) *adjective* Honest; real; genuine: *Our feelings are **sincere**.*

skel•e•ton (skĕl´ ĭ tn) *noun* The framework of bones in the body of a human being or an animal having a backbone: *People training to be doctors study **skeletons** to learn about human bones.*

slick (slĭk) *adjective* Very smooth and slippery: *After the rain, the sidewalks were **slick** so we had to step carefully.*

reunion

The word *reunion* was formed by joining the Latin prefix *re-*, meaning "again," with the Late Latin word *unire*, meaning "to unite." Therefore *reunion* means "to unite again."

section

oō **boo**t / ou **ou**t / ŭ **cu**t / û **fur** / hw **wh**ich / th **th**in / *th* **th**is / zh **vi**sion / ə **a**go, sil**e**nt, penc**i**l, lem**o**n, circ**u**s

G7

slope (slōp) *noun* A stretch of ground that slants upward or downward: *The **slopes** on the hills behind our house are great for sledding.*

sniff (snĭf) *verb* To breathe in through the nose quickly and with a soft noise: *Mom likes to **sniff** the fresh herbs from her kitchen garden.*

sol·id (sŏl´ ĭd) *adjective* Hard, firm; not hollow: *Those statues are made of **solid** ice.*

spine (spīn) *noun* Part of a plant or animal that sticks out with a sharp point: *Porcupines are covered in prickly **spines,** or quills.*

spot (spŏt) *verb* To see, find, or locate: *The bird watchers **spotted** a huge woodpecker on their walk.*

store (stôr) *verb* Put away for future use: *Squirrels **store** acorns for winter.*

suc·ceed (sək sēd´) *verb* To carry out something desired or tried: *We will **succeed** at reaching our goal if we all work together.*

sur·viv·al (sər vī´ vəl) *noun* The act or fact of staying alive: *The family's **survival** is due to the firefighters' quick action.*

temperature

T

tank (tăngk) *noun* A container for holding or storing liquids or gases: *Divers always check to be sure that their **tanks** are filled with air.*

tem·per·a·ture (tĕm´ pər ə chər) *noun* Hotness or coldness as measured on a standard scale: *The **temperature** is warmer in the sun than in the shade.*

ter·ror (tĕr´ ər) *noun* Very great fear: *I screamed in **terror** as the roller coaster turned upside down.*

through·out (thro͞o out´) *preposition* In, to, or through every part of: *We walked **throughout** the city and saw all the sights.*

thump (thŭmp) *verb* To hit in a way that makes a low, dull sound: *The children **thumped** their feet to the beat of the music.*

thun·der·ous (thŭn´ dər əs) *adjective* Loud and rumbling: *A **thunderous** noise woke everyone up.*

ă rat / ā pay / â care / ä father / ĕ pet / ē be / ĭ pit / ī pie / î fierce / ŏ pot /
ō go / ô paw, for / oi oil / o͞o book

trop·i·cal (**trŏp** ĭ kəl)
adjective From or typical of
the tropics, the warm areas
of Earth near the equator:
*Mangoes and bananas are
both **tropical** fruits.*

twist (twĭst) *verb* To wind
together to form a single
strand: *I watched as the
woman **twisted** her long hair
into a beautiful braid.*

U

un·cov·er (ŭn **kŭv´** ər)
verb To reveal or remove the
cover from: *Workers digging
the tunnels are **uncovering**
many objects from an earlier
time.*

un·ex·pect·ed (ŭn´ ĭk **spĕk´**
tĭd) *adjective* Taking place
without warning: *We gasped
when we heard the **unexpected**
news.*

V

voy·age (**voi´** ĭj) *noun* A
long journey made on a ship,
aircraft, or spacecraft: *The
astronauts will remember their
voyage into space for the rest
of their lives.*

W

wil·der·ness (**wĭl´** dər nĭs)
noun An area in a wild,
natural state in which there
are no people: *You might see
unusual animals and plants in
a **wilderness**.*

voyage

ōō b**oo**t / ou **ou**t / ŭ c**u**t / û f**u**r / hw **wh**ich / th **th**in / *th* **th**is / zh vi**s**ion /
ə **a**go, sil**e**nt, penc**i**l, lem**o**n, circ**u**s

Acknowledgments

Main Literature Selections

The Albertosaurus Mystery: Philip Currie's Hunt in the Badlands by T. V. Padma. Copyright © 2007 by Bearport Publishing Company, Inc. All rights reserved. Reprinted by permission with Bearport Publishing Company, Inc.

Boy, Were We Wrong About Dinosaurs! by Kathleen V. Kudlinski, illustrated by S. D. Schindler. Text copyright © 2005 by Kathleen V. Kudlinski. Illustrations copyright © 2005 by S. D. Schindler. Reprinted by permission of Dutton Children's Books, Division of Penguin Young Readers Group, A Member of Penguin Group (USA) Inc., 345 Hudson Street, New York, NY 10014. All rights reserved.

Dog-of-the-Sea-Waves written and illustrated by James Rumford. Copyright © 2004 by James Rumford. All rights reserved. Reprinted by permission of Houghton Mifflin Harcourt Publishing Company.

The Journey of Oliver K. Woodman by Darcy Pattison, illustrated by Joe Cepeda. Text copyright © 2003 by Darcy Pattison. Illustrations copyright © 2003 by Joe Cepeda. Reprinted by permission of Houghton Mifflin Harcourt Publishing Company.

The Journey: Stories of Migration written by Cynthia Rylant. Text copyright © 2006 by Cynthia Rylant. Reprinted by permission of The Blue Sky Press, a division of Scholastic, Inc.

Excerpt from *Judy Moody Saves the World!* by Megan McDonald, illustrated by Peter H. Reynolds. Text copyright © 2002 by Megan McDonald. Illustrations copyright © 2000 by Peter H. Reynolds. Reprinted by permission of Candlewick Press, Megan McDonald and Santillana Ediciones Generales, Spain.

Life on the Ice by Susan E. Goodman with photographs by Michael J. Doolittle. Text copyright © 2006 by Susan E. Goodman. Photographs copyright © 2006 by Michael J. Doolittle, except where noted. Reprinted by permission of Millbrook Press, a division of Lerner Publishing Group, Inc. All rights reserved.

Mountains: Surviving on Mt. Everest by Michael Sandler. Copyright © 2006 by Bearport Publishing Company, Inc. All rights reserved. Reprinted by permission of Bearport Publishing Company, Inc.

Excerpt of "My Smelly Pet" from *Judy Moody* by Megan McDonald, illustrated by Peter H. Reynolds. Text copyright © 2000 by Megan McDonald. Illustrations copyright © 2000 by Peter H. Reynolds. Reprinted by permission of Candlewick Press, Megan McDonald and Santillana Ediciones Generales, Spain.

Excerpt from *Sarah, Plain and Tall* by Patricia MacLachlan. Text copyright © 1985 by Patricia MacLachlan. Reprinted by permission of HarperCollins Publishers.

"Stopping by Woods on a Snowy Evening" from *The Poetry of Robert Frost* by Robert Frost. Copyright © 1969 by Holt, Rinehart and Winston, Inc. Reprinted by permission of Henry Holt & Company.

A Tree Is Growing by Arthur Dorros, illustrated by S. D. Schindler. Text copyright © 1997 by Arthur Dorros. Illustrations copyright © 1997 by S. D. Schindler. Reprinted by permission of Scholastic Press, a division of Scholastic, Inc.

Credits

Photo Credits

Placement Key: (r) right, (l) left, (c) center, (t) top, (b) bottom, (bg) background

3 ©Jonathan Blair/Corbis; 4 (tl) ©Scott Stewart/AP Images; 5 (tl) ©Commonwealth of Australia/Australian Antarctic Division; 6 (bl) ©Stapleton Collection/Corbis; 6 ©Dan Rafia/Aurora Photos/Getty Images; 7 (tl) ©Stocktrek Images, Inc./Alamy Images; 7 (b) ©Francois Gohier/Photo Researchers, Inc.; 10 ©Getty Images; 10 ©Tony Anderson/Digital Vision/Getty Images; 10 ©digital vision/Getty Images; 10 ©Tom Grill/Corbis; 11 ©Javier Larrea/Age Fotostock America, Inc.; 11 ©Paul Hurst/Alamy Images; 11 ©Digital Vision/Getty Images; 11 ©Barry Mason/Alamy Images; 11 ©HMH; 11 ©G. Baden/zefa/Corbis; 13 ©Alamy Images Royalty-Free; 39 © Corbis/SuperStock; 40 ©StockTrek/Photodisc/Getty Images; 53 (br) ©Rubberball/Getty Images; 54 (tc) ©Natural History Museum, London/Alamy Images; 54 (tr) ©Richard T. Nowitz/Photo Researchers, Inc.; 54 (br) ©Alamy Images; 54 ©Jonathan Blair/Corbis; 54 (bc) ©David McNew/Getty Images; 55 (tl) ©David McNew/Getty Images; 55 (tc) ©Mark Wilson/Getty Images; 55 (tr) ©Richard Nowitz/Corbis; 55 (bl) Michael Andrews/Earth Scenes; 55 (bc) ©Blickwinkel/Alamy Images; 55 (br) ©Photolibrary New York; 57 © PhotoDisc/Getty Images; 60 (l) ©Eva Koppelhus/Dinosaur Research Institute; 61 (t) ©Philip Currie/Dinosaur Research Institute; 62 (b) ©Richard Nowitz, Photographer; 63 (b) ©Richard Nowitz, Photographer; 65 (t) ©Gail Mooney/Corbis; 66 (br) ©Bettmann/Corbis; 68 (b) ©Richard Nowitz, Photographer; 69 (t) ©Michael S. Yamashita/Corbis; 69 (br) ©Philip Currie/Dinosaur Research Institute; 71 (cl) ©Richard Nowitz, Photographer; 72 (b) ©Museum of the Rockies Montana State University; 73 (t) ©Carlos Goldin/Photo Researchers, Inc.; 74 (b) ©Richard Nowitz, Photographer; 77 Photodisc/Getty Images; 78 ©Alamy Images Royalty Free; 79 ©Bert de Ruiter/Alamy Images; 80 ©Jonathan Blair/Corbis; 80 (br) ©Jonathan Blair/Corbis; 80 ©Photodisc/Getty Images; 81 (cr) ©Scott Camazine/Photo Researchers, Inc.; 82 ©Photodisc/Getty Images; 82 (br) ©plainpicture GmbH & Co. KG/Alamy Images; 83 (cr) © Jason Edwards/National Geographic/Getty Images; 83 ©Jonathan Blair/Corbis; 83 (cr) ©Scott Camazine/Photo Researchers, Inc.; 87 (br) ©Jack Hollingsworth/Getty Images; 88 (tc) Jonathan Kirn/Getty Images; 88 (tr) Beverly Joubert/Getty Images; 88 (bc)